MELANOMA MELODRAMA

Also by Chuck Myer

Gilroy's Old City Hall: 1906 - 1989
Backstages: 1981 - 1990
Chanukah Gold
Placer County: An Illustrated History

MELANOMA MELODRAMA

A Medical Memoir

Chuck Myer

Melanoma Melodrama. Copyright © 2008 Chuck Myer. All rights reserved.

This is a memoir, a work of creative nonfiction.

This edition published by
Umbach Publishing
6966 Sunrise Blvd., #263
Citrus Heights, California 95610

For information: info@umbachconsulting.com or 916-733-2159

ISBN: 978-0-6152-0681-3

Photographs by Chuck Myer except as noted:

> Chapter 2. American Gothic, photo by Kevin German, *Sacramento Bee*, copyright 2005. Adapted by the author with thanks to Kevin German and the *Sacramento Bee*. Used by permission.
>
> Chapter 11. Head and neck scars.
>
> Chapter 13. Alicia Parlette faces the gamma knife. Chronicle photo by Penni Gladstone, used with thanks to the Chronicle.
>
> Chapter 17. The Cancer Package (montage).
>
> Chapter 25. Chuck in Milan.
>
> Chapter 26. A new scar.

Lyrics from "Live Like You Were Dying," by Tim J. Nichols and Craig Michael Wiseman, copyright © Alfred Publishing, used by permission.

Contact Chuck Myer at cmyer@comcast.net

4/27/08

Acknowledgments

The medical books tell us how we're supposed to get well. But sometimes it's the personal stories we tell each other that communicate the way to survive and heal.

The events in this book took place in late 2005 and to late 2007. After I was diagnosed with melanoma cancer, I received strong support from several others, including Mark Wendland, Denis Eucalyptus and Steve Durbin, who had been through the same diagnosis and recovery. What I later experienced seemed remarkably close to what I had been told, and I found it much easier to cope, having heard their stories, rather than battling the unknown alone.

And so, I wish to tell my story, in the simple hope that it, too, will help a future melanoma patient grapple with the sudden awful realities brought on by a seemingly benign spot on one's skin.

Much of what I've written is in the present tense; these chapters were originally designed as newspaper columns written in real time, that readers might experience these events as I did.

Encouragement and suggestions were provided by Marjie Lundstrom of the *Sacramento Bee,* and Richelle Cochran at the Sutter chemo ward, and Lawrence Spann and the Sutter Health *Literature, Arts and Medicine Program*, and its Sutterwriters group.

Suellen Rowlison, R.N., a retired public health nurse, was there for me twice as my medical advocate/liaison. And I give eternal thanks to my many doctors and their support people who really did save my life: Dr. Kali Eswaran, Dr. Randall Ow, Dr.

Nitin Rohatgi, Dr. Margaret Parsons, radiation doctors Susan Lee and Bruce Jones (with assistance from Drs. Leibenhaut, Suplica, and Lodgson), and Dr. John K. H. Yen, Jr.

The United Methodist Church has been very supportive of my needs during this ordeal. I'm thankful. And finally, I thank my family, Becky, Holly and Timothy, Becky's family, my brother Dale, niece Alison and my mother Flo. They were and are my inspiration to go on living.

A note on privacy:

I realize I have lost most of my own. But I guess I fell into this long ago, during my years of serving as a columnist, journalist, and public information officer, and living in the "stained-glass fishbowl" (in a clergy family). My medical troubles were subsequently reported in many publications, pulpits, and websites, with various levels of accuracy.

I hope those to whom privacy is still important will have their diseases in easy-to-hide places. It was not so for me; my head and neck were opened three times, for the entire world, figuratively or literally, to see . . .

Contents

Acknowledgments v
1. Diagnosis: Trouble 1
2. "I'm Going to Beat This!" 5
3. The Word is Out 9
4. Actions and Reactions 13
5. The Long Wait 17
6. "The Blame Game" 21
7. "Cancer Central" 25
8. Healing 29
9. Pre-Op 33
10. Op 37
11. Post-Op 41
12. Frankenstein 46
13. Alicia 50
14. Clinical Trials and Tribulations 54
15. Wish Upon a Star 57
16. View from the Chemo Ward 60
17. The Cancer Club 64
18. Spiderman 68
19. Inject Thyself 73
20. That's Depressing 76
21. Testimony 80
22. Triumph 84
23. No Scintigraphic Evidence 89
24. Randomness and Religion 92
25. Italy 94
26. Brain Drain 101
27. A Better Person 111
2008 Update 115
About the Author 117

1. Diagnosis: Trouble

I want to tell you about something I've had on the back of my mind. It turned out to be a tumor.

It was on the scalp on the back of my head. At first I thought it was just a bad patch of dandruff. My wife asked why I was scratching my head a lot.

"It's nothing."

Funny how those little moments come back to haunt you.

When it wouldn't go away, I thought I must have been victimized by one of those melodramatic maladies you see on commercials on late-night cable television.

Eczema! Psoriasis! (I wasn't even sure what those were.)

I thought there might be some kind of ointment on the pharmacy shelf that might help me. I found one for psoriasis, and started reading the small print.

"Warning: This product contains chemicals that are known to cause cancer."

Right.

Funny how those little moments come back to haunt you.

I really didn't want to bother the doctor about a patch of dandruff. But when it bled, I knew I needed to go in. One of the subordinate doctors in the office was on duty that day, a woman doctor I had not seen before. I felt a sense of relief that my main doctor wouldn't be there when I came in with such an embarrassingly trivial complaint.

She looked at it and said I had an infected hair follicle. (I was to learn that this is often the first diagnosis by general practitioners who see melanomas on the scalp.) So I trundled off with a week's worth of antibiotics.

"Come back in a week," she said.

Did that week make the difference? I'll ask myself that the rest of my life.

Because when I returned a week later, my main doctor, Kali Eswaran, an East Indian man of few words, took one look and declared, "Skin cancer. Lie down on the table. I'll cut it off." And he left the room to get a knife.

When a person first hears the word cancer in relation to himself, there is a certain shock wave. My wave was disrupted a few seconds later by the two young, female office assistants who were sent in to "prep" me for the minor surgery. They were giggling about cell phones and boyfriends, oblivious to the human sitting there trying to absorb the "C" word. Their only mission was to start cutting hair to get it out of the way of the doctor's blade.

The doctor returned. In went the first needle to numb the scalp, and off came the offending circle of skin. In a few minutes, it was over, and so was the problem, according to the doctor. He had it pegged as squamous cell carcinoma. But of course he would send the oval-shaped chunk of my scalp off to the lab just to make sure. They showed it to me in its little jar. Like the foreskin after the Jewish ceremonial *bris*.

Interesting what the doctor said a few days later, when I came in with a new complaint. Now this soft-spoken man is from India, and is named for a Hindu deity, and his office advertises, "Urdu spoken here." So I didn't expect this when he felt the new lump on the side of my neck:

"JESUS!" he exclaimed.

Somehow optimism remained in the room. The lump could be normal drainage from the wound, settling in the lymph node.

"Come back in a week and let me feel it again," he said.

Did that week make the difference? I'll ask myself that the rest of my life.

Optimism had disappeared a week later. The doctor's office called and left a message that was more like a summons.

"You are to appear in the doctor's office at 9 a.m."

"Sounds like bad news," one of my friends said that evening.

"No, I need to go in anyway, so the doctor can check the wound. He needs to tell me the lab results himself— not one of the cell-phone-toting candy-stripers who make the phone calls."

It's the 21st of September, like the Earth, Wind and Fire song I'll never forget.

You are to appear in the doctor's office at 9 a.m.

So why is it that when I do show up at 9 a.m., the young medical assistant is sitting me up on the tissue-papered bench, and asking me, "What is the reason for your visit?"

"Well," I hear myself reply, "I'm here to find out whether or not I have cancer."

"Oh, the doctor will tell you that in a minute. But first we need to check your pulse and blood pressure!"

Right. I think this would be a good time to check those, since I'm probably setting the Guinness World Record in both categories.

Close to it.

Then the doctor walks in and looks me in the eye. The man of few words.

"You have malignant melanoma. Clark Class IV."

I know what melanoma is. And the way he's enunciating the "Four" pretty much tells me that "Clark Classes" don't go up to XCLVIII or something like that.

In the next few blurry minutes, he walks me to his office, and gives me the names of the first three other doctors I am to see.

"You are going to be a very busy man the next few weeks."

Right.

Everything blurs. I try to write down what he's saying but my pen runs out of ink.

"Here." He hands me one of those fat pens adorned with product brands that the medical salespeople give out as free samples.

"Sandostatin LAR Depot," says the pen. "Octreotide acetate for injectible suspension."

Right.

What's scary is by the time this is over, I might know what that means.

That pen is still in my pocket. I will be using it to fill out countless medical forms in the weeks to come. And to write these words.

And so begins my journey into the bowels of the medical bureaucracy as I engage a battle with cancer at age 51. It starts with a whirlwind of blood and urine tests, chest X-rays, MRIs, PET and CAT scans, fine-needle biopsies and consultations with medical oncologists, surgical oncologists, and radiation oncologists, and a few dermatologists thrown in for good measure.

And all because of a bad patch of dandruff.

Funny how those little moments come back to haunt you.

2. "I'm Going to Beat This!"

It's like I'm in a detective thriller, and I have just been handed the first clue: a piece of paper with handwritten names on it. And the clock is ticking.

My doctor has just told me I have cancer; now he's dismissing me with this list of oncologists and other specialists. It's out of his hands now.

"Do you have their phone numbers?" I stammer.

"They'll call you," he answers ominously.

Stunned, I walk out of the office and out to my car. The late morning sunshine continues unabated, in some kind of twisted, ironic insult.

Melanoma is triggered by the sun. How could something so warm and friendly have given me cancer?

"Sunshine on my shoulders makes me happy.
Sunshine on my shoulders makes me cry."

I look at the piece of paper in my hand, and suddenly I'm reliving the most common doctor-patient stereotype since Hippocrates. I can't read the doctor's handwriting!

OK. Concentrate. One thing at a time. He also gave me lab referrals. The blood lab is close by, in Rancho Cordova. I can start there.

"Have you been fasting in preparation for your blood test?" the nurse asks.

"No, can't say that I have. This sort of just came up."

The nurse pulls out the needle. I would be seeing a lot of those in the weeks to come. She could tell I had had a lot of blood drawn from each arm.

Chuck Myer

"I'm a 7-gallon blood donor," I brag. Then I suddenly realize my blood donor career has just come to a screeching halt. Now I may need to be a recipient.

I need to get a chest X-Ray. I pick a place in Carmichael from the list of "routine diagnostic radiology imaging centers" only to find a sign there, "We don't do X-Rays here." Wasted trip. Time is precious, and I'm spinning my wheels. Alone.

I drive by a little church, whose pastor is taking pastor calls for my wife, who is away. He's not expecting this. I pull into the parking lot.

The secretary asks about the bandage on my arm. "I'm a blood donor!" I lie. "Is the pastor in?"

Do I ask him why God is punishing me? No. I don't have time to waste. What I need from him, besides a quick prayer, is this: I have formulated a plan, and I have to run it by a confidential professional who can make sure I'm behaving rationally.

My wife and daughter, a high school senior, are away, visiting college campuses in Southern California. It'll be several days before they can be back to help me (and I'll need their help aplenty later on). But if I tell them the diagnosis today, it will totally destroy their ability to concentrate on their mission: touring USC and UCLA. So I need to keep this ugly news to myself for at least two days. I can't tell others before I tell my wife—and I have a lot of living to do in the next 48 hours (including a musical performance that very evening). My pastor friend sadly agrees, and sends me off with a blessing.

I need to go home and think. I need a computer; and a phone directory.

Deciphering the doctor's handwriting leads me to the first proof that God indeed has a sense of humor. My surgeon's name is Dr. Ow.

Oh, well, at least I can pronounce it. (Unlike the next name on the list, which is illegible, unpronounceable, and, as it turned out, badly misspelled.)

I soon learn that everyone calls him "Dr. O." I don't know if that's the correct Asian pronunciation, or if his is the first two-letter name in history that needs to be shortened. But to his eternal credit, Dr. Ow has already left a message on my machine; and he left his *personal pager number* for me to contact him. Wow. He wants me in his office right away for a flexible fiberoptic laryngoscopy (translation: I have to drink walrus feces and get a long snake stuck up my nose.)

Dr. Ow's level of concern tells me one of two things. Either he's the world's greatest doctor, or he's telling me that my time is short.

"I'm not going to lie to you," says Dr. Ow, looking at my chart. "This is a thick tumor. 5.25 millimeters. This is serious."

More tests are scheduled.

That night I dream about the apocryphal call from the doctor who says he has bad news and worse news: "The bad news is that the tests show you have 24 hours to live."

"Doctor, I can't believe it!" I say. "What could be worse than that?"

"I didn't have time to call you yesterday."

The next day I wait by the phone. Nothing.

The third morning I wake up at 4:30. A thousand "to-do" list bullet points dance the tango across my brain. It makes more sense to just do them than to just think them. It's clear I'm not going back to sleep any time soon.

It's time to be proactive, not reactive; to take control of this situation.

I start a list. For the first time in my life, I'm going to need

Chuck Myer

a cell phone. And I've got to find that unpronounceable oncologist and camp out on his doorstep until he admits me as a patient.

I need a folder to put all of my medical records in. Something that uplifts my spirits, too. I select one with a rainbow print, and I also find a matching nametag, hand-lettered by my wife.

I go out to the porch to pick up the morning paper, the *Sacramento Bee*, and there's the inspiration.

A neighbor had left me the back issue of the *Bee* that prominently featured my photograph in the celebration of the 75th anniversary of Grant Wood's "American Gothic."

I grab the scissors and paste, and soon I'm looking at the colorful file I would take with me to dozens of medical offices in the weeks to come.

Framed by a rainbow is the photo of me, holding the celebrated pitchfork, and proclaiming:

"My name is Chuck. And I'm going to beat this!"

3. The Word is Out

Some people can't even bring themselves to say the word "cancer." Many try to keep it a secret when they have it. But I had a hard time pulling it off for just two days: the two days I had to wait before I could tell anyone about my diagnosis.

For one thing, it's hard to keep it a secret when your head is bandaged. And I have already had gauze strips on the back of my head, stitches on my face and a band-aid on my neck.

For a while, I had a quick retort to fall back on. Since I had a bit of notoriety from the *Sacramento Bee* article in which I was pictured imitating "American Gothic," I told people that I had had "a pitchfork accident."

I briefly considered trying to delay (or "embargo") the news. But two minutes after I entered the cancer clinic for the first time, I ran into our church's lay leader.

So there will be no secrets. Actually, I think the worst nightmare would be to try to continue to relate to everyone in my life as if everything is OK.

It's not OK. There's a lump in my neck, and it's getting bigger. A pathologist stuck a "fine needle" into it and pulled out cancer cells. So *no*; *not OK*.

Now I have an appointment at a place called the "Nuclear Medicine Center." Hope I don't have a meltdown.

As I'm leaving to go there, a sewer main ruptures in the corner of our front lawn and starts spewing up raw sewage in a fountain of brownwater and toilet paper.

Today's lesson from the Hebrew Scriptures can be found in

the Book of Job.

I'm going to be late. I'm getting a PET scan, and here I am dialing the Public Works emergency hotline, hoping that my new cell phone won't disrupt the energy beams from the huge doughnut-shaped robot I'm about to be sent into on a conveyor belt.

I go to a dermatology center, where they examine the rest of my skin (in places I didn't know I had). They scrutinize suspicious moles and take another minor biopsy on my face. More work for "Igor" in the laboratory.

* * * *

No, things are not OK. I cannot pretend they are. People need to know.

I have already called my wife and daughter who were traveling—they're on board. And my 10-year-old son is taking the news well.

But when my mother finds out, she may need more medical help than I do. Previous health crises in our family have sent her into a tailspin.

So my first priority is to tell her in person—slowly, carefully, so she doesn't assume the worst. That means I need to get to the Bay Area to see her—and I need to make sure the news doesn't arrive there, via cable modem or wireless phone, before I do.

I succeed.

So now it is OK—OK for the news to follow its own course along the information superhighway.

Meanwhile, I need to educate myself quickly, to de-mystify melanoma, so I can explain it to my friends. I learn that a study reported in the *Journal of the American Academy of Dermatology* found that well-educated white-collar men have the highest

Melanoma Melodrama

risk of developing it. "Researchers surmise that a pattern of many months of little skin exposure (a result of working indoors) with occasional overexposure and sunburn (such as that acquired at sunny resort vacations) may be responsible."

Right. I represent that remark. Although I don't remember the fancy resort part.

People have misconceptions about melanoma. They ask me: "Do you work out in the sun?" (I don't.) "Do you play golf?" (Well, nothing under 100.) "Are you in pain?" Actually, no. I'm on sick leave, but I feel fine.

Everyone knows someone who had melanoma.

"My late uncle had it." Thanks.

But there are survivors, too. I need to join a support group. I need to know what I'm in for. Soon I will meet melanoma sufferers who have lost a finger, an eye, or their sexual function.

Mostly it looks like it'll be at least a year of pure grief. With the major surgery and a long course of treatments, I'll be out of commission for quite a while.

So I'm trying to finish off the chores in the yard, but the Mormons *and* the Jehovah's Witnesses come by. They buttonhole me while I'm on the ladder. How do they know? Is there some kind of list? *"Vulnerable man on 1600 block of Church Street—soul needs saving before cancer surgery..."*?

A little good news finally arrives: the biopsy on my face is benign. The pathology report comes back with a romantic sounding result: *"Venous Lake."* It's just a blood vessel. So far the cancer is confined to my lymphatic system.

Dr. Ow wants to do surgery ASAP, so I decide to get my hair cut short, out of his way if he needs to do a skin graft. I'm probably going to lose hair permanently anyway from the radiation.

Chuck Myer

But I need a barber who won't get squeamish about the scabs and tumors. The newspaper says they're cutting hair for donations down at the school track during the "Relay for Life" benefiting the American Cancer Society. Perfect.

Mary Ann Becker cuts lumps of my graying hair as teams of joggers and walkers circle the track for 24 hours to raise funds and cancer awareness. The emcee is extolling everyone to wear a hat and sunscreen to ward off skin cancer—the most common type. *Roger that.*

I join the walkers for a lap around the track, passing through an ominous gauntlet of *luminarias* (candles in sand-weighted paper bags) that are adorned with the names of cancer victims and survivors.

Melissa Etheridge. The feminist singer surviving breast cancer.

Linda McCartney, who died of it.

Alicia Parlette. The young copy editor who is writing about her fight against alveolar soft part sarcoma in the San Francisco Chronicle.

And suddenly I stop in my tracks.

Chuck Myer.

There's one with my name on it.

I guess the news has gotten out.

I keep walking. Only then do I wonder: did my candle say *Victim* or *Survivor*?

4. Actions and Reactions

How do you tell someone you have cancer? Point-blank? Slowly and obliquely? Face-to-face over coffee? Over the phone? By e-mail? Or worse yet, by bulk e-mail?

I've had to make that call over a hundred times.

At first I worried most about my immediate family's reaction. In fact, I had delayed telling them while they were on a road trip visiting college campuses.

But we're a pastor's family, and pastors' families are used to dealing with crises. My wife immediately came to the conclusion that I would be all right, and that the problem would be quickly eliminated. Therefore, she adopted a "life goes on as usual" approach, and the kids quickly closed ranks behind her in that resolve.

Meanwhile, other friends came to the opposite conclusion, and assumed I would die before the year was over. A few booked flights to come see me "one last time."

How will someone react when you tell them you have cancer? Well, as you might expect with humans, the reactions are across the board. Some gasp in horror at the mention of the word. Others are *ho hum* about it.

A lot of it depends on the age of the person who has it. At 51, I'm still young enough for purists to see the injustice of it all, but I know I don't engender the emotional outpouring of sympathy extended (appropriately) to someone like the lovely 21-year-old woman in our church choir who got thyroid cancer, or 23-year-old Alicia Parlette (mentioned earlier).

In my particular case, I have a choice on how I present the

information. There are at least four wordings I can choose. And in some cases, I make the choice according to the level of reaction I want to create—usually to minimize the impact. (I am not above maximizing the impact if it works to my advantage.)

I can say I have "skin cancer." I had, of course, used this terminology prior to the actual biopsy result. When used with the word "skin," the word "cancer" seems to lose a great deal of its usual fear in the human mind. I work a lot with retirees, and in groups of older folks, discussion of "skin cancer" is often blown off as one would dismiss mosquito bites or teenage zits. My older friends who hear only that I had skin cancer have a tendency to chuckle to themselves as they think such a "youngster" might blow something that trivial out of proportion.

I can say "I have melanoma." My diagnosis of melanoma can be used in place of the "the C-word" when I think it may be appropriate. Some people don't really know what it is and whether it's serious or not. "Melanoma" is a bit more accepted in the lexicon than other medical jargon terms like "sarcoma" or "carcinoma," which sound worse. To those who are used to skin ailments, "melanoma" often engenders in the listener the concept of survival—of a small skin "eruption" or bad sunburn that has been caught early—too early to be referred to as cancer.

I can say "I have cancer." The Big C. It always sticks in the throat. When someone hears me say it, they instantly flash back to their dear departed grandmother or aunt, and a thousand other memories flood over them.

I can say "I have malignant melanoma." Now that one really sounds like I'm at death's door. Malignant *anything* sounds bad. But it gets the point across that it's not just a mole that can be removed and forgotten about. "Malignant cancer" is another derivation that makes it sound to my friends like now is the time they better return all the stuff or money I loaned them.

The real bone-chiller is "metastasize." That one word sounds more like a death sentence than anything else. ("Don't forget about Lance Armstrong!" I remind them. His cancer metastasized and he came back to win the Tour de France seven times!) Like all of the other terms, this was true in my case: my melanoma had metastasized to a lymph node in my neck. But, at least in the case of melanoma, that's just the first step. Doctors refer to it as a "local" or "regional" metastasis. If it spreads to other internal organs, that's called "distant" metastasis. But to the general public, the very use of the word tends to make eyes glaze over in horror—the rest is too technical.

So I choose my words carefully. I know if I'm talking to someone face to face, they can see I'm standing, that my vital signs are vital, when I give them the news. Someone on the other end of a phone or cable can't see that.

It depends on the personality of the person. I told my brother right up front over the phone. But for my mother, I did it in person and took all day doing it, to create the absolute minimum shock to her already beleaguered system.

I also use the kid gloves with other friends who have lost family members and expect the worse. Tears flow too easily with these folks. The worst sub-types in this category are those who throw up their hands to heaven and take on the aura of Job. They ask why God is punishing *them*, by striking down another of their friends!

Some cut me off—like they can't handle this right now— and in a few cases I haven't heard back from them at all.

But revealing my condition is not always a downer. There really are optimists and survivors out there, and there are others whose cases are much worse than mine.

Chuck Myer

Most people, of course, are repulsed to see the tumor sticking out of my neck. But others are intrigued, and occasionally I meet up with someone from the medical community who has a true academic interest in my symptoms.

I'm in a Starbucks, and I see a whole group of medical students boning up (pardon the pun) for an exam. And I'm thinking, is this too weird for me just to go up to them and say, look, you can see it—it's a cancerous tumor. Would you like to feel it? Would it help you someday making your own diagnoses?

No, that is too weird. So I just sit here and sip my coffee. And write some more in my journal.

5. The Long Wait

When you're facing surgery, particularly cancer surgery, you feel like you're on the uphill climb that will never end. How appropriate that the patron saint of cancer patients, Lance Armstrong, is best known for his uphill climbing of Alpe d'Huez in the grueling Tour de France.

On the uphill side you feel helpless. In my case, no medicines are being prescribed. You just have to wait. Wait for a phone call and a date with the surgeon. Wait for the lump in your neck to get bigger. Wait for a new one to appear.

I want to do something about it! Should I go places? When I do, I feel like I'm in a scene from "Dead Man Walking"—especially if people around me don't know what's going on.

Shouldn't I be resting? Conserving my energy? Changing my diet?

Instead I'm running around like the proverbial chicken with its head cut off (not a good analogy for someone facing head and neck surgery). I'm trying to get everything done that I would be doing if things were normal, and everything that I would need to do during the months ahead when I'll be out of commission.

Meanwhile there are more delays. The first tentative date for surgery was a mere nine days after my initial diagnosis. But that was way too ambitious: there wasn't even time to get all the preliminary tests done and results back: lab work, chest X-rays, PET and CAT scans, dermatology exams, and deep-needle biopsies.

Scheduling surgery is very complex. My surgeon knows

time is of the essence, and tells me he's willing to do my surgery at night or on a weekend—but he needs to have the assistant he's used to working with, and has to coordinate schedules with him. (That sounds like a good idea to me.)

So the surgery is pushed to a new date, some 27 days after my initial diagnosis. That's another two and a half weeks of agonizing waiting.

And life goes on.

Do I maintain peace and quiet? No, I take off like whirling dervish.

Like one of Pavlov's dogs, I start going down the "honey-do" list from summer and anticipate it ahead into the winter: I'm clearing gutters, changing track lighting, scrubbing out the spa, fixing gates—everything I've been putting off or ignoring. All the things a husband and father should be doing (or should have done already). And all the while I'm secretly celebrating the fact that, for these few days at least, I still have full use of my limbs and body.

In fact, while my close friends and family members are paralyzed with fear, I'm running around being twice as productive as I ever was.

During these long waiting days, do I just do everything I would have normally done? As if nothing was wrong?

Should I tell every single co-worker and casual business associate? Or if I do, will I become "damaged goods," unable to get future contract work if word gets out? Will I have trouble securing future employment if my health benefit is going to be a big liability?

How about social engagements? Block parties? Church? Music rehearsals?

I have to pick and choose what to do and where to go.

Melanoma Melodrama

Here's one not to be missed: the afternoon before the surgery is the date of my son's 11th birthday party. We have the 3-5 p.m. shift at King's Skate roller rink. Another surreal experience: I'm standing in the strobe lights as kids on in-line skates whiz by me. I can skate free as the birthday dad, and I enjoy skating. But what if I get injured? I want to arrive at the hospital through the pre-registered desk, not through emergency.

But what if something goes wrong in surgery? Would this have been my last chance ever to go skating? And I passed it by? Do I seize the day? Or wait in the wings?

Other parents are hanging around the cake and presents. Some I've just met. Some I've known for years. Do I tell them what I'm going through? Not the ones I've just met, surely. They're just here to pick up their kid—they won't even remember my name. I decide not even to mention it to the others. It's my last chance for normalcy—to be with people who don't know. But that was a mistake: I find out later that one of the other fathers was a cancer survivor himself who had been on Interferon . . . I could have learned from him.

So here I sit, silently, on the edge of a skating rink while my boy and his friends glide gleefully by. I'm reminded of the scene from Act III of Thornton Wilder's "Our Town," when Emily Webb arrives in the purgatory-like graveyard of chairs in the Grover's Corners cemetery. She asks the stage manager if she can see what's happening with her family, before her untimely death.

"Can I go back in time? To a special occasion maybe?"

"You can, but it's too painful," says the stage manager. "Because you know the future."

"Can't I pick a happy day?" she pleads.

"No!" shouts Mother Gibbs. "At least pick an unimportant

day. The least important day. It will be important enough."

"Can I at least choose a birthday?" says Emily. The stage manager nods. "Then I choose my 12th birthday."

And so, like Emily, I'm looking at a child's birthday party through the dark mirror, holding the knife and cutting the cake while knowing that in 24 hours I will be unconscious, and the knife will be entering my own neck.

Will I make it to my son's 12th birthday?

6. "The Blame Game"

It's 3 a.m. Sleep is elusive after you've been handed a diagnosis of cancer. And melanoma, the most insidious form thereof, really leaves you clueless in the search for answers.

Now I don't know if I'm awake or asleep. I don't know if I believe it, but dream analysts say that everyone who appears in your dream is actually you. Or some manifestation of you. Except your mother. She's the real McCoy.

In the haze, I can see into a room. I'm looking through one-way glass into an interrogation room. There are seven suspects standing against the grid, holding numbered cards. They're telling me I have to pick one of the suspects.

The man holding up the number "1" is a 60-year-old CEO type in a patriotic tie and a business suit. He fidgets in his chair. He's clearly uncomfortable, like he has the most to lose.

There is a lot more confidence on the face of the 60-year-old Filipino woman holding the "2." She keeps looking over at the dark-skinned man from India holding the number "3." He has a face that's hard to read. He wears a stethoscope around his neck and a smile just one shade too close to being a smirk.

The weeping, red-eyed 80-year-old woman with the "4" measures only 4'9" on the height grid. I remember her at 5-feet even. Of course, I remember her as being taller than me. *Spinal stenosis* has taken its toll.

Next to her, "5" and "6" are holding hands—a couple in their early 50s. He looks concerned; she looks confident. He has a bandage on his neck.

At position number "7" is another 80-year-old, bald on top

with long white hair and a flowing beard. He doesn't look American. His skin is fair, and seems to be of Celtic, Teutonic or even Aryan stock. Sometimes you can just tell if a person were to start speaking, it wouldn't be in English. He doesn't look well.

The bailiff has all seven turn 90 degrees for another photograph, then he snakes the line into the hall and over to a preliminary hearing room, where I, now sitting as judge, can question them.

"Oyez. Prelim hearing for the assignment of guilt. Judge Chuck presiding."

(Not only does my name pop up in my dreams, it rolls by in the credits at the end.)

On my judicial bench I have textbooks and computer files at my fingertips. I address #1, who is still fidgeting.

"Your company's factories have high emission levels that are breaking down the ozone layer. Melanomas and skin cancers are increasing at an alarming rate."

"With all due respect, your honor," says the defense attorney, there isn't enough evidence to prove that cause and effect. Surely that exonerates him."

I guess he's right.

"Doctor," I ask #2. "When you saw the back of my head, you said it was an infected hair follicle—and sent me off with only antibiotics."

"But I told you to come back, so he could see it," (she nods towards #3)—"and take a biopsy if he thought it necessary."

"Surely that exonerates her," says the defense attorney.

"Yes, but even then," I say to my family doctor, #3. "You never mentioned the possibility, or even the word, *melanoma*."

"I didn't think that's what it was," he replies matter-offactly. "But I did an incisional biopsy as soon as I saw it, and sent it to the lab."

"Surely that exonerates him, your honor," says the defense attorney.

"I've been warning you about melanoma all your life," wails #4.

"Yes, Mom, you have."

"Let the record show," says the judge, "that melanoma has been shown to be hereditary."

"I inherited a lot of moles from you, Mom. And fair skin."

"But I never had melanoma! Neither did your late father."

"Let the record show that he came from Northern European stock, and not much is known about his ancestors who lived near the German-Polish border."

Unseen, the white-haired old man, #7, is leaving the room.

"But I always told you to put on sunscreen!"

"Yes, Mom, you did."

"I always checked your moles," she pleads. "And when you got married, I asked *her* to."

She gestures to the woman holding #5.

"Surely that exonerates her, your honor," says the defense attorney.

"I watched his moles," says my wife. "But this wasn't a mole. It was under all his hair. I don't even see how sunlight could get under there."

"I couldn't have expected her to examine my scalp every night!" says #6, who is also me. "I ...never checked hers."

"Surely that exonerates her, your honor," says the defense attorney.

"Don't blame her. It's my own fault," continues #6. "I admit it. I'm the one who exposed myself to the sun."

"Whose son?" demands the judge.

"No, no, no! *The* sun! I went to the beach in Santa Cruz in 1971 and didn't even take the Sea and Ski… I knew I had fair skin. I should have figured it out sooner. I was too embarrassed to tell the doctor. But I just thought I was using the wrong shampoo. If Dr. #2 didn't recognize it, how could I? I couldn't even see it!"

"Surely that exonerates him, your honor," says the defense attorney. "There isn't enough evidence to attach any responsibility to any of the six defendants."

"Only six?" I ask. I look; there is nobody at #7.

Out of the window, I can see them putting a stretcher in the back of a limo. The white-haired man lies on it, still. The limo is black.

"I know what you're thinking," whispers the defense attorney to me. "But don't even think about trying to blame it on God. That defense never works."

The bailiff stands. "Oyez, oyez. The judge will now make the declaration of guilt."

The bailiff rings the courtroom bell.

But it's the alarm clock.

Now I'm awake. And alive.

And I need to hurry. I'm due at the Cancer Center at 8:30.

7. "Cancer Central"

The Sutter Cancer Center is an imposing structure—linked to Sutter General Hospital by a breezeway the way an appendage linked Eng and Chang, the original Siamese twins.

The architecture is classic, and obvious effort has been made to make the facility feel soothing and supportive to the fractured and fragile human beings who enter its gates.

The building, completed in 1989, is named for Richard B. Buhler, a trustee for Sutter Community Hospitals from 1979-86. There's history on this site, as you can see by the cement marker in the courtyard—featuring a capital "S" with one end of the "S" emblazoned with the head of a deer. The emblem was originally placed over the entrance of the original Sutter General Hospital on this very site in 1923.

A memorial pool and fountain greet pedestrians. The air of serenity tries to mollify the fast pace of the traffic and city life a few yards away. The dedicatory plaque honors Marlene Chriss Gerspach-Warnes, who was a supporter of research and education programs for ovarian cancer. In fact, the whole building seems to be filled with dedicatory plaques – featuring smiling bronze portraits of dead people who fought this disease before it ultimately beat them.

I'm here today to figure this place out.

My first mistake on my first visit was to park on the street and feed the parking meter. I didn't realize there is valet parking for all cancer patients. I can see it there, but it didn't occur to me that I was entitled to it—I'd be taking away a parking space from a cancer patient! It still wasn't sinking in. I don't have a handicap plate, I don't know if I'm supposed to tip, and I'm still quite ambulatory, thank you very much. Maybe later.

I walk in the door for the first time, like "Mrs. Robinson":

"Stroll around the grounds until you feel at home. Cu-cu-ca-chew."

There's nobody at the information desk, but there is a directory, so I look for the name of the oncologist (the name that was almost undecipherable on the first referral slip.) It turns out that he's a SCHMO.

That is to say he was one of the doctors in the Sacramento Center for Hematology and Medical Oncology (SCHMO).

So, I'm thinking, I'll be spending my time shuttling between Dr. Ow and Dr. SCHMO. Wonderful.

"Can I help you find something?" A handsome, helpful woman is offering me assistance.

"I think I've found it—third floor. But I'll accompany you to the elevator!"

As we walk, I confess it is my first visit. Maybe the first of hundreds. As we get in the elevator, she sees my motivational poster ("My name is Chuck, and I'm going to beat this!"). She smiles and says that attitude is the most important factor. The door opens at the second floor. A friend of mine steps into the elevator! She's a Sutter employee, and she is suddenly very impressed with me, because, unbeknownst to me, I'm chatting it up with *the Head of the Foundation.* So my friend assumes I'm in the building to go to the top floor for a meeting with the top brass.

Then we get to the third floor: Oncology. And I exit, alone. Her face is crestfallen, because now she suddenly realizes why I'm really in the building. And, bound by confidentiality rules, she knows she must keep silent.

Melanoma Melodrama

I walk on to the SCHMO waiting room. I can see right away that things are different. Not just a magazine rack here—there are books, and jigsaw puzzles and research computers. People obviously spend a lot of time here: several have small suitcases, lunches and coolers.

The receptionist looks like a battle-ax, but she is cheerful and helpful.

I meet some chemo patients— "chemo cousins" who have forged bonds with one another during months of treatments. One even gives me advice as to which chemo chair to avoid – seems there's a draft in the corner. I explain I'm not getting chemo (yet)—I haven't even had the surgery. It's my first visit. They look at each other knowingly.

Bill has cancer throughout his body. So does Josefina. Arturo is here for his last treatment. He's been declared cancer-free. It's like graduation day for him. But Arturo doesn't seem happy—perhaps he feels guilty since he knows some of his friends will never "graduate" the way he is today.

Bill is wearing a "LIVESTRONG" bracelet popularized by Lance Armstrong. Several others are, too. *Note to self: I need one of those.*

After I fill out all of the required paperwork and set up my first round of appointments, I start checking out all of the information in the brochure racks. There are lots of support groups—for caregivers, for dance therapy, for writers, for people from different religious backgrounds.

There is a sign advertising free hats for cancer patients. At first, I laughed. They were matronly women's hats. But the volunteer said they had them for men, too. So, I took one: a knit cap that covered my surgical scars. (It looked so much like a *yarmulke* that the valet parking crew wishes me "Happy Hanukkah!")

I picked up the annual report, and flipped it open. Sure enough, there she was. The "angel" who was helping me find my way on my first day: Katherine M. Keeney. Executive Director of the Sutter Medical Center Foundation.

Nice to have friends in high places.

In October, which is Breast Cancer Awareness Month, the hallways and display panels were filled to overflowing with gorgeous quilts of all kinds, donated by various groups around the state for an annual auction to raise funds for breast cancer.

In the strangest quirk of fate, I found a notation in my calendar that made my jaw drop. I had scribbled in for November 4: "Sutter Cancer Center" "Sing for the Cure." At the time I wrote those words, I didn't even know where the building was. But I was scheduled to sing there with an ecumenical chorus group on the day the quilt auction was held.

Who would have guessed by the time that date rolled around, I would be scheduling myself for daily treatments in this very building?

And on November 4, I joined with other singers from around the community, standing beneath dozens of beautifully displayed quilts, "Singing for the Cure." With a new sense of urgency.

8. Healing

During my cancer ordeal, a lot of friends have been concerned that I would not stop enough of my various activities to put sufficient focus on my health. One of the great cards I have received shows a dog giving commands to an ill human who obviously needs to go back to bed.

"Sit." "Lie down." "Stay."

And then on the inside: "Heal."

There are cancer cells in my body. So what do I do about it? Is healing still possible?

Obviously there is always a surgeon who assumes it's his job to rip out the little devils. But are there things that I should be doing in the meantime to stave off this menace? On the one side, there's the established medical community that's giving me long lists of hoops to jump through—their hoops, their way. And on the other side there's the whole spectrum of holistic healers, brimming with a lot of new age suggestions that all my doctors would probably just scoff at. Do I have to choose one or the other? Or is there a happy medium?

I learn that healing comes in many forms.

"You need acupuncture," says my sister-in-law. "And green tea."

I'm not sure about those needles, but I promise her I will drink green tea.

"Yoga," says a neighbor. "Chakra cleansing."

Another neighbor tells me to try shark cartilage enemas.

I decide to stick with drinking green tea.

"You need Reiki," says a trusted friend. (*What?*)

Chuck Myer

So, OK, I'm going to need to do some research. I learn that Reiki is a Japanese word for Universal Life Force Energy given to an ancient form of natural hands-on healing by a Dr. Mikao Usui, who studied healing phenomena of the world's greatest spiritual leaders in the late 19th century. Reiki practitioners profess to actually heal themselves and others with the laying on (or near) of hands.

Next comes a whole stack of audio tapes—designed to wrap my mind around what's happening to my body. One is an "Affirmation Loop." Others are a mind/body relaxation CD from Susie Mantell, healing facilitator, and "Think and Get Well—A wellness guide" from pop guru Andrew Weil. These will put me in touch with my inner self. I guess the worst that can happen is you fall asleep listening to them.

My range of acquaintances is unusually large, due to the variety of my work and leisure interests. So I have friends in all walks of life, and all religions. I was, indeed, comforted to be told by various friends and relatives that diverse groups of people all over the world, it seems, are praying for my health:

A friend of mine in Congregation Beth Shalom went to Yom Kippur services and added my name to the *Mishabayrach* prayer with the Hassidic/Chabad Rabbi.

The monks at the Redwoods Monastery at Whitehorn, CA have been instructed by another contemplative friend to include my name in their prayers.

A special round chanted just for me by the devotees in the temple by Vatsnava Maha Vishnu Raga Ji Prahbu and the devotees of Sri Krishna at the Temple of Gold in New Vrindaban, West Virginia.

Many of the health professionals I have been visiting are from India and Russia, so I figure that I have some Hindu and

Orthodox gods aligned on my side already.

In the Christian pantheon, I have friends in many denominations beyond my own. We United Methodists are pretty low key when it comes to overt healing, but more evangelical folks have been well known for their revival tent healing services over the centuries. Steve Martin's performance in the movie "Leap of Faith" comes to mind. Should I avail myself of those types of opportunities? I mean, this is, after all, my life I'm fighting for here.

In an uncanny piece of timing, I learn that a number of my friends at a large church in Granite Bay are planning a healing service—the very night before my surgery.

Coming in to officiate at the service is Bishop David Mullen of the Sierra Pacific Synod of the Lutheran Church. During the liturgy, he will oversee several of the time-honored ceremonies designed for healing – the anointing of oil, the laying on of hands. Communion by intinction is also offered, along with prayer partner counseling.

The choice of communion is ironic. In my own tradition, United Methodism, grape juice is always used, in part, to avoid any problems with alcoholics in recovery who might be at the communion rail. But Lutherans use the real stuff—in fact, the *good* stuff.

A couple of times, members of my church tradition who have attended Lutheran services here were caught off guard by the strong wine they used. One sip can be enough to knock a reformed person off the wagon.

This hadn't been a problem for me; fortunately, I had never inherited my father's predilection towards alcoholism. And as an aficionado of fine wine, I even developed an appreciation for their rich *vin santo* communion wine in previous visits.

But this time, though, I had another consideration: I had strictly cut off alcohol from my regimen as soon as I found out I had cancer. And here I was just hours before surgery: I didn't want even a drop to get in the way of effective anesthesiology, etc.

So I had to find an alternative, quick. Fortunately, for this special service, someone had realized this problem exists, and a grape juice option was offered in the corner.

Written prayer petitions are placed in a large copper bowl, and at the close of the service, I am chosen to be the one to take the large bowl from the nave and walk it slowly forward to the chancel for its blessing by the bishop.

I am honored to do so.

One moment still haunts me. When the bishop placed his hands on my head, surely he couldn't have known that the very place where his fingers were touching me was the place where cancer first entered my body?

Could he?

9. Pre-Op

A man is going to pick up a knife and cut my throat open. And he's going to earn thousands of dollars for doing so.

After that, comes the hard part. He's going to start carving into my head. Down to the skull. Somewhere along the way, he's going to decide whether he will carve a chunk out of my leg and sew it into my head.

But first he's going to open up my neck, and take out a fig-shaped tumor that has been jutting out for all to see these past few weeks. It used to be a lymph node, before it gave its life to science.

He's going to remove over thirty other lymph nodes, because they may have been infected with the same cancer cells. Later, in the lab, they'll be sliced, diced and dissected under a microscope to see if they are cancerous, or if they were actually still good lymph nodes that I might have wanted to use the rest of my life.

I'm not sure which answer I want to hear about that one.

The chart at the end of my bed sums it all up. It says that today I'm getting a "Right selective neck dissection and wide excision of right scalp lesion."

Other than that, I should have a pretty good day.

I am surprisingly upbeat going into surgery. Cancer survivors have told me that it's actually a relief to get this point—the point at which you're finally able to start taking progressive action to solve the problem.

Up until now, the problem's just been getting worse. Now is when it's supposed to start getting better.

Chuck Myer

So I'm actually smiling heading into Mercy San Juan Hospital. I've got my ducks in a row; I even have an advance health care directive, signed, witnessed, and on file. I have already pre-registered the week before—so no paperwork hassles today, hopefully. They have my regular medications on file, too, and will be administering them to me over the next several days. And I have been fasting since last night (including passing over the communion wine at the healing service).

A couple of years ago I visited my brother-in-law here. He had had heart surgery done by (I'm not making this up) a Dr. Slaughter. So he can now appreciate the fact that my surgeon is Dr. Ow.

The only surgery I've had up to this point has been oral: adenoids out in 1959, wisdom teeth out in 1979. So I don't really know what to expect. I don't recall ever having had the "honor" of having a catheter, so that's going to be another new experience.

I'll miss the whole show, of course. I've been telling everyone "I'm taking the day off." Dr. Martinez, my anesthesiologist, will see to that. The burden will fall on my wife, who will hold the lonely vigil in Mercy San Juan's surgical waiting room, surrounded by her mother and sisters, and another female friend. Funny how very often it's the women who fill these support roles. It was all women who waited at the tomb—the male disciples had scattered themselves far and wide. But perhaps I stretch the analogy too far.

My wife's family was Catholic. Emphasis on the "was." This is ironic, since this hospital is operated by Catholic Healthcare West ("committed to furthering the healing ministry of Jesus, and to providing high-quality, affordable healthcare to the communities we serve"). My wife left Catholicism when it became clear the priesthood was unavailable to her as a career option—in fact, so was the coveted position of altar boy.

But evidently Catholics are pretty good at running hospitals.

I'm interested in having a non-family member in attendance, too, so we've arranged for my friend Suellen, a retired nurse, to be there as an advocate/liaison (someone who can translate medical jargon if necessary). This turned out to be one of the best ideas of the day. Suellen is keeping a journal, writing down all the medications, the options, the details of the surgery, even the shift changes of the nurses.

A surgery nurse comes into the pre-op space, which is basically a bed surrounded by a curtain.

"We're going to give you a steroid to reduce inflammation. OK?"

"Won't that dash my hopes for a major league baseball career?" I respond.

She smiles.

A chaplain friend comes in, and offers a prayer. How did he find me?

The surgeon comes in to go over the last-minute details. He had warned me about the possible loss of a nerve, and he is deadly serious about it now. It appears that the tumor may have invaded it, and its loss would give me weakness in my arm movements and quite possibly chronic pain. This is one of the last things he reiterates before the surgery, as if he's afraid I won't remember.

I have authorized him to do a skin graft if necessary. The lack of skin covering on my skull may need to be fixed up with some fresh flesh from my thigh or elsewhere. Of course, there would be no more hair growth there. Oh, well, it's close to where most men get a bald spot anyway.

The trip into the surgery center was surreal. The series of wide double doors open to a push on a metal disk by the attendant behind me, so they look like they're opening automatically—like the inner chambers in one of Disney's Fantasyland adventures for kids. The gurney becomes the boat traversing the underworld caverns of the River Styx—and I've been given just enough drugs to retain the surrealism.

They keep asking me my name.

They keep asking me which side of my body the surgery is going to be on.

Why? Aren't they sure?

Did somebody sue you about that? Their dialogue seems drawn from the paperwork of previous malpractice lawsuits.

The bulging tumor sticking out of the right side of my neck, plain to see, should be the only necessary clue here. They even mark it.

X marks the spot.

Then Dr. Martinez, the anesthesiologist, puts something under my nose.

"This'll take the edge off," he says.

And then, like Sgt. Schulz, I know nothing, I see nothing, and I feel nothing.

10. Op

Thanks to the anesthesiologist's magic elixir, I'm out like a light bulb. But through the magic of creative writing, I'm floating overhead in a literary out-of-body experience, watching the drama as it unfolds below.

They're wheeling my unconscious body into the surgical suite. It's about 1 p.m. Now comes the long day's journey into night.

An array of medical equipment is arranged next to me—I'm straining to see what the tools are and wondering what they are all used for. The surgeons will be working near some large blood vessels, so they have equipment ready in case they need to do a blood transfusion. I get a certain sense of justice from that realization, since I have donated blood over 50 times since 1981. Maybe it was all in preparation for this moment?

Dr. Ow seems to be in control, and working well with his team. Now it's time to begin the "right selective neck dissection."

After the preparatory work is done, they set to work on my neck. A large incision is made, the skin is opened, and the work begins. The one large infected lymph node is "palpable"—which means it could be felt even before surgery, so it's the first to go. The one below it goes next.

When a palpable node isn't so obvious, dyes are used to find the "sentinel node"—the one the cancer cells attack first. But in my case, that isn't necessary.

Lymph nodes are grouped in clusters in five places in the neck area. The doctor plans to take out three clusters, leaving the farthest two. It's impossible to actually count the number of lymph nodes he removes until they get to the lab. The doctor estimates that he's taken out 15-30 others. The full story won't be known until the lab results come back. (Maybe not even then, if you don't know the jargon. The later microscopic diagnosis shows: *"a) lymph nodes, right cervical, level 2-5, modified radical neck dissection: metastatic malignant melanoma to one (levels) of thirty-three cervical lymph nodes (1/33) w/ negative for extracapsular extension."*)

The hours are ticking off on the clock as the lymph nodes come out. In a miraculous bit of work, they have spared the nerve in the neck. However, there is a lot of fluid drainage—there may still be some temporary damage from two drains that have been surgically inserted into my shoulder and chest.

The neck skin will be raised and open from the neck bone to the front of the jaw. The neck won't need a bandage, except at first to catch drainage. Ointment will need to be applied at home.

As they sew up my neck, I'm looking down from my out-of-body vantage point, seeing snippets of my life flash before my eyes. For some reason, I'm flashing back to junior college, where I am president of the honor society, Alpha Gamma Sigma, and I'm working on the design of a logo for the club.

There's a new surgical tool in the pantheon of cancer treatments called the gamma knife. It isn't actually a knife at all – it's a series of very precise dosages of radiation directed at a particular spot.

But now I can see why these diverse thoughts are surfacing in my brain: the foot-long scar from my ear to my shoulder is the reverse of the lower-case Greek letter *gamma*.

At 6:10 p.m., the phone rings. One of the surgical nurses

answers it. It's my wife, Becky, trying not to sound worried. The nurse assures her that I am indeed still in surgery.

At 6:35 p.m., a guy in blue scrubs and surgical attire goes through the double doors and emerges into the surgical waiting area. A group of women, my family members, are asking him about Dr. Ow's patient. He tells them the doctor is just closing up the neck now. And then they will start in on the scalp.

Dr. Ow is getting tired. But he still needs to excise my scalp lesion to make sure there is no more cancer in the original site. That's problematic, because there isn't much skin up there to work with. On the scalp, he cuts off the necessary margin, using a very scientific procedure: he measures off two centimeters with his thumbnail. The tissue is saved for later analysis in the lab. But he can't quite close the incision. The scalp is too tight.

The doctors are authorized to do a skin graft in case this happens. But the skin graft isn't a good idea, it turns out, because the graft would have little chance of survival if I'm going to be having radiation later. So what to do?

The winning suggestion comes from, amazingly, the anesthesiologist! Dr. Martinez suggests making two relief incisions elsewhere in the scalp, off to the sides. Sort of like a "tummy tuck" for the head. Dr. Ow later admitted that he might have thought of this himself if he hadn't been so tired. In the meantime, he shows his appreciation for his colleague's suggestion.

The incisions work; they're able to close the gap. There's an oozing bandage now on the site, and a pressure stocking cap, but it looks like I'm coming out of it OK.

At 7:35 p.m., a scrub nurse with a blue bonnet comes out to say that Dr. Ow is closing the scalp now and he will come out soon to speak with my family.

At 8:03 p.m., Dr. Ow emerges. He is elated as he tells Becky the good news about the nerve in my neck. They are obviously relieved.

At 8:10 p.m., Lisa and Amy, my sisters-in-law, leave. They have their own families to attend to.

At 8:25 p.m., Dr. Ow tells Becky she can go into the recovery room area when I am more awake. They have given me some Demerol, and an IM (intramuscular) injection for nausea. I'm pretty sweaty coming out of surgery. Of course, so are the doctors. Dr. Ow leaves for the evening, exhausted.

At 8:45 p.m., the RN named Rick says the recovery phase is almost over.

At 9:03 p.m., I emerge from the surgery suite on the gurney and am transported to the fifth floor, room 5536.

At 9:25 p.m., my wife visits me in my room. I am reportedly sweet and mellow. And my first words are "Thank you."

11. Post-Op

Somebody is saying to me: "The surgery is over." What I'm hearing is the old joke from the end of the Catholic mass: "The service is over. Thanks be to God."

This is weird. I can't remember waking up in a hospital bed before.

"Hmm. My neck seems to hurt." OK, well that's a start. I am just coming to after head and neck surgery. It's time to take inventory. Yes, there are large bandages on my neck, and a pressure cap on the back of my head.

But I don't feel any injuries anywhere else. Yes! That's good news. That means they didn't have to do a skin graft! So my legs and limbs are intact, at least.

And even better, I soon learn, they have saved the nerve in my neck—the one the surgeon was afraid he'd have to cut. Imagine my surprise… this is the best news of all. The surgeon had warned me about the loss of that nerve, because it appeared the cancerous tumor had invaded it, and its loss would give me chronic pain and weakness in my arm movements.

There are some new additions to my chest, which now has plastic tubing coming out of it. I look like a half-human cyborg. There are two punctures, with tubes leading to plastic bulbs that are filled with ugly-looking fluid. To install these Jackson-Pratt drains, the doctors actually have to make separate stab wounds in my chest, and then suture the tubes to the skin. They're connected to plastic bulbs that are squeezed and emptied of air content. When the bulb recoils, it creates a vacuum and sucks blood or fluid from the wound, in order to prevent hematoma (hemorrhage or internal bleeding). So OK, this'll take some getting used to.

There is an IV tapped into a vein in my arm, and a catheter. I've never peed through a catheter before.

There's something weird on my legs. Compression stockings, with pumps attached to the calves of my legs to aid in blood circulation and avoid clotting.

OK. Now for a visual scan of room 5536.

There are folded origami paper cranes on the shelf! A gift from my wife. And flowers in the room, too. This is a Catholic facility, so the omnipresent crucifix is here also.

There's a sign that reads, "It's OK to ask your health care provider to wash his/her hands." Right. I'll make a note. I'm sure they'll enjoy that.

They have given me some plastic balls to squeeze, and a breathing apparatus called an incentive spirometer to use to keep my lungs clear of any residual anesthesia.

My friend Suellen has done yeoman's duty—staying way beyond the visiting hours to help me get oriented. She has taken notes on all the medical terminology, and has even briefed the nurses that come in for a shift change as to what the previous nurses had been doing.

The special role—the medical advocate—is a wonderful thing. I really recommend it, if possible for anyone going into surgery. Having a clear-headed medical professional on your side is a Godsend.

The first day I am just elated. I am so happy to have that tumor out of me that I'm practically giddy.

I'm even being a smart-ass when the phone rings.

"Melanoma Ward! Will you hold?"

I assume I'll be on some kind of soup and applesauce diet

here, but no: They bring me three square meals a day, without saying a word about it. They serve me, and I don't have to feel guilty about it. I just have to eat it.

I seem to have forgotten how to use a straw.

I have a Russian nurse named Tatiana. She runs a tight ship. The nurses from the other shifts have warned me about her.

My wife and kids had gone out for Chinese and sneaked me in a fortune cookie. Tatiana probably would have resigned in disgust if she learned of this malicious bending of the hospital dietary regulations.

A woman across the hall has been letting out this dreadful moan ever since I've come to. It's hard to remain optimistic with "Moaning Myrtle" going off like a fog horn 24 hours a day.

I cut my hand on a surgical staple in my scalp. Ouch.

Dr. Ow comes for a visit to see how I am doing.

"Talk to me. How are you feeling? What hurts most?"

I have to learn about pain levels. They keep asking me, is it 1 through 10? (I'm tempted to quote from "Spinal Tap" and tell them it's at "11.")

Actually, I am hoping to stay off pain medications. This causes some discussion from the doctor and nurses. They tell me not to take aspirin products or Motrin. I surrender and agree to take some Vicodin.

I get a lot of calls and visitors. Many of them are clergy friends. They are our friends, but they often don't remember how to visit a friend in the hospital—they are too used to making official clergy calls. So they wrap it up after 10 minutes by offering a prayer, and it's over.

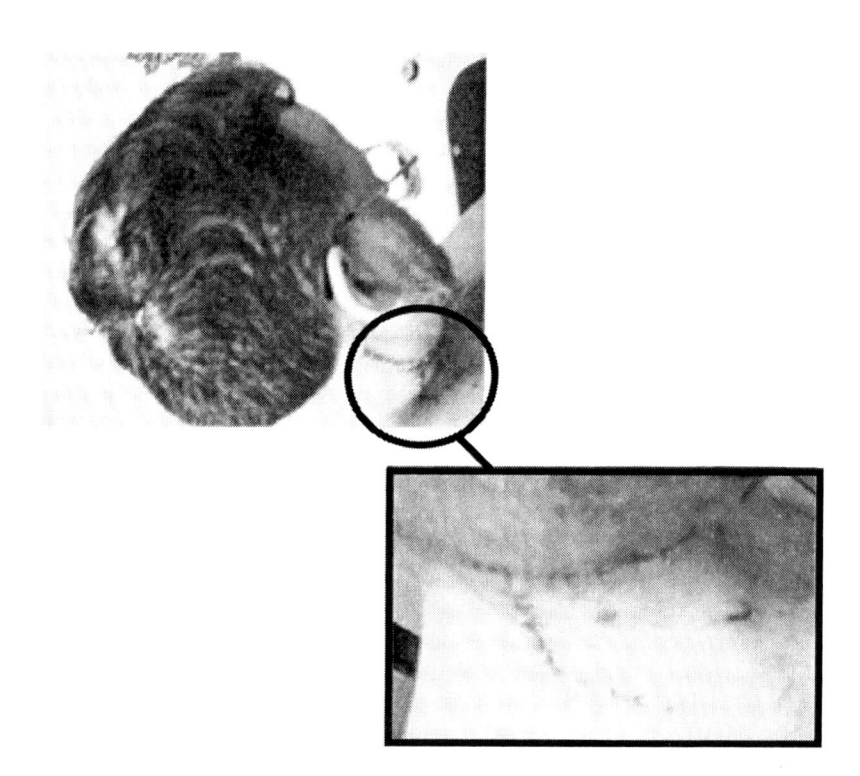

I am eventually relieved of the catheter, and Tatiana gets me up to go to the bathroom on my own power. I also get a real gift: some pajama bottoms. This is nice. After a day of the hospital gown, this is a great improvement.

But on the second day, I don't feel as good as I did the day before. Reality is starting to set in. Now it's nearly time to go home, Jackson-Pratts and all, but ironically, I feel worse than I did before. Am I scared to leave the womb-like safety of the hospital?

My brother is in town, and he volunteers to be the one to drive me home. This is a good idea, because he has a large vehicle which rides smoother than our family car. I'm still pretty fragile. My wife will follow behind.

And soon I'm home. It feels good to just sit in the rocking

chair and do nothing.

As I rock, I mourn the death of my lymph nodes, removed liked yesterday's trash, though all but one were healthy, functional, functioning. Thirty-three lymph nodes that served me well for fifty years. Their battle ends. Their retirement is nigh. I should have given each of them a gold watch. And the medal of honor to the one that made like Audie Murphy and sacrificed itself by absorbing the cancer.

The surgery is over. Thanks be to God.

12. Frankenstein

It's late October. I am home now, and I have to face the biggest challenge of all.

The mirror.

It's not a pretty picture. I'd cry, but it hurts if I do.

I have three parallel incisions in my head and a large crater where tissue was removed from my scalp. Two incisions were made to relieve pressure in the remaining scalp, which needed to be stretched to cover the piece that had been removed.

I also have a three-pronged "flap" incision from my right ear to my larynx down to my shoulder. All of the above are being held together with about 50 awful-looking surgical staples. I also still have tubes that are draining pink fluid out of my chest.

In short, there is little question who will be chosen for the coveted part of Frankenstein this Halloween.

I'm obviously going to have a Bad Hair Month. In fact, I still might lose my hair to radiation. Oh, well, I can still play Daddy Warbucks in the musical *Annie*. In fact, my theatrical friends would approve of the fact that I got the "scalp tuck" instead of the skin graft.

My head still needs a lot of work, and I'm not much help, because I can't get there from here.

I can do virtually everything necessary in running a household, except for two things: I can't give birth, and I can't see the back of my head. So now the importance of the latter requires a daily regimen of ointment on my scalp wounds, a messy business in any case, particularly if I try to do it myself. So I'm learning to lean on my wife as she learns to assist me in daily scalp and hair care.

The intensity and the location of the surgery has impacted our relationship a bit.

Up until now our marriage has always been characterized by mutual respect for each other's professional careers. We have maintained our marriage as a partnership of equals. This is the first serious illness we've had to deal with, and it does throw the delicate balance off-kilter when one partner needs to be nursemaided on a daily basis.

We're able to make light of it, however, by calling it the daily "sálon" – with the emphasis on the first syllable, as pronounced by David Spade in a Saturday Night Live sketch that poked fun at men's hair care. Every day I need "sálon" treatments with gauze and Bacitracin ointment. She does these for me regularly, with a good spirit. I also need to put ointment on my neck wound and the staples, but I can do that pretty well by myself.

All this ointment gets pretty slimy on the bed pillows, so I have to stick with the industrial hospital pillows for a while. Night sweats are also a problem. Head injuries are problematic in that way.

We went to a Halloween party at the church. There were zombies and witches and the whole motley crew. But I became a particular attraction to some of the teenagers—they started coming up to get a close-up view of my neck. (The staples are quite obvious.)

"Wow! That's cool. Who did your make-up? It almost looks real."

I left them to wonder.

There are many follow-up visits to see the surgeon, Dr. Ow. Each time a few of the surgical staples can come out. Most of them are scheduled to come out on, you guessed it, Halloween.

I'm in his office, and the doctor yells out to his assistant, "I need a staple remover!"

To clarify, I yell out, "A *medical* one—not the kind on your desk!"

There are some elusive staples in my head. I can feel them, but I can't see them. And the doctor can't see them either, evidently, because every time he thinks he's gotten them all, I find another one later.

Now I'm worried that one of them will screw up the brain scan (MRI) that I'm scheduled to have.

They have prescribed Vicodin, and occasionally I "treat myself" to one, just so I can take a break from the pain. But Vicodin causes constipation, too. And so here's another prescription to soften stools—so one thing keeps leading to another, and another.

Here's what I'm learning: When you're under 50, the physical highlight of your day is an orgasm. When you're over 50, it's a good bowel movement.

I know the road to recovery will be long. The scar looks just like the Greek letter *lambda* (*gamma* reversed). My neck and shoulder are so sore, but I'm told massage is dangerous—you don't want to be messing around with lymphatic fluids right now. So it's going to be at least six weeks before anything resembles "getting back to normal."

The pathology report isn't back yet—they removed between 15 and 30 lymph nodes from my neck that need to be tested to see if they removed all the cancerous tissue.

People are kind when they see me. The Frankenstein joke works OK as an icebreaker. A few are surprised that I haven't already lost my hair and beard. In fact, the beard is already covering over part of the surgical area. There are also going to be huge amounts of scar tissue on my neck. And the hearing in my ear is being affected, although I don't know whether that's permanent.

One day my cell phone rings. It's the surgeon. He has the pathologist's report.

And he's calling on a cell phone? Surely it can't be bad news or I'd be called into his office!

And I'm right.

On the scalp, there is no "residual neoplasm"—no additional cancer tissue in the additional margin they removed after the first biopsy. And of 33 lymph nodes removed, only the original one with the tumor showed cancer cells.

This is about the best possible outcome to be hoped for.

I call my family together and give them a hug.

I may look like Frankenstein, but I feel like Superman.

13. Alicia

In 2001, I met David Parlette at a spiritual retreat, and soon learned, in a prayer circle, that his wife was dying of cancer. We did the best we could to provide support for him during that weekend. We continued support from afar until the inevitable happened the next year.

This kind of thing happens.

But what shouldn't have happened, not to Dave, not to anybody, was having to face the news, soon after, that his daughter had cancer, too.

Dave's wife died in relative obscurity. But soon thousands of people knew of the family's dilemma. Why? Because Dave's daughter, Alicia, the 23-year-old copy editor for the *San Francisco Chronicle,* began writing about her cancer journey in the pages of that newspaper. The series became quite popular, and spawned a website and a published book.

Alicia was diagnosed with alveolar soft part sarcoma, a rare form of cancer that she had evidently developed in high school. The series detailed how she learned that she has a rare cancer and that it has spread from a tumor on her hip to her lungs, breast and pelvic bone. Her best hope for treatment, like mine, is the drug Interferon. Her doctor also ordered MRI scans of her hip and brain to see whether the cancer was spreading. Following that, a discovery of cancer cells in her brain led to the use of the gamma knife technology to remove two small tumors. The procedure was duly recorded and presented in the pages of the *Chronicle.*

"*Alicia's Story,*" as the series came to be known, has had a

Melanoma Melodrama

strong impact on readers across the state. But it had a triple impact on me, in a much more personal way. First, I already knew the family, and the extended church family where the Parlettes worshipped. Second, I was discovering I had cancer myself. And third, I, too, am a journalist, interested in documenting my cancer experience for readers to share in the experience.

When someone has such a common bond with you, something special can happen—you instantly hug them when you first meet. This was the case the day I met Alicia.

It was at her family's church in Granite Bay. It was a special evening healing service, a first for that congregation, and one for the most part based on her experience, and in many ways for her benefit. She had become the focus of a great deal of prayer and energy in that church, and the prayer circles and support groups that had sprung up around Alicia grew into a full-fledged healing service with the Bishop of the Synod in residence to lead the service.

Ironically, the service was the night before my own cancer surgery.

So I felt a bond of commonality with Alicia as she kneeled at the altar at that healing service. She was not alone—a photographer from the *Chronicle* was there, too, recording this part of her story – her appearance at the healing service — for the omnipresent series.

Alicia laughed when I told her what I wanted to do.

"I want to copy you," I said.

Never mind the pun on her title (copy editor). What I meant was that, I, too, wanted to write about my experiences battling cancer. Writing is very therapeutic, especially in a case like this. But I'm talking about a lot more than journaling, or recording "my cancer thoughts" in a diary. I am talking about sharing my actual experiences with the reading public, in real time, and allowing them to accompany me on the journey, the end of which is still unknown.

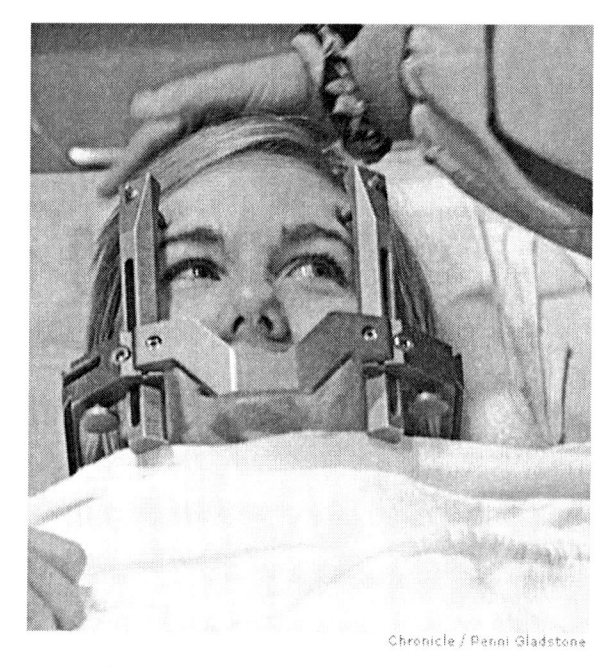

Alicia prepares for the gamma-knife

This is what Alicia is doing, and doing well. As a journalism intern, she had wanted to have the opportunity to write, and she surely has the opportunity now. Her columns are filled with self-revealing emotion, often very personal revelations about her fears, her paranoias, and her fractured personal relationships with friends and family members. She also details her visits with not only oncologists but psychologists, as well. She discusses what it is like to be straddling her two worlds, cancer and non-cancer.

The readers of the *San Francisco Chronicle* have responded in many ways, making inquiries, sending cards, making donations to various related charities, etc.

My story is a little different. I'm not young, like Alicia, so the heart-rending nature of her situation—a beautiful young woman who has not yet had time to marry and raise a family—obviously does not apply. But I do have experience as a writer, and I might be able to shed some light on the whole process as I go through it in such a way as to help someone who has to go through it later.

The columns I write aren't really like Alicia's—hers are more "stream of consciousness," moving fluidly from one topic or event to the next, with heavy doses of "feelings" included alongside. Mine are more categorized: I try to stay on the same topic, mostly for my own sanity.

Ultimately, my initial efforts were thwarted. My proposal for a series of newspaper columns was ultimately rejected, but not right away: the editors sat on it for six weeks—a lifetime when you're in cancer treatment. So by the time they decided against it, the topical, real-time aspect had all but shriveled up and died.

Am I envious of Alicia? Am I wishing I had the publicity she's getting for other reasons involving my own ego? No. I wish her well. She knows and I know that neither of us would have chosen this "assignment" for ourselves, even if a giant step forward in a journalism career might be a result.

Still, I keep writing in my personal "cancer thoughts" journal, even if that's as far as it goes—the therapeutic value of writing about one's illness is well-established. In my darkest days, I wrote one chapter per day, and gave them to a willing set of readers—the nurses in the chemo center!

14. Clinical Trials and Tribulations

There comes a point after each cancer diagnosis where a patient has a difficult choice to make. Since cancer research is always ongoing, and always changing, there is usually some sort of clinical study being conducted somewhere that could prove to be the cure to your particular form of cancer.

Or not.

There's a problem with being in any clinical study—up to half of the participants are going to receive a "placebo"—a dose of sucrose or something that is not the medicine being tested, merely so patients receiving the new drug can be compared to other patients who aren't.

A recent comic strip dictionary defined "placebo" as: "A pill with no side effects other than death."

While all patients receive some sort of assistance and advice, a person could potentially lose his or her battle with cancer because of the luck of the draw. When you have cancer, you really hate to be throwing your fate in with a pair of dice (even though it was chance and fate that got me into this mess in the first place).

Recently, actor Michael J. Fox played a cancer patient on the television series "Boston Legal." This was poignant enough, since Fox famously suffers from Parkinson's Disease, and watching him work so hard to control his tics and tremors on camera makes it hard to concentrate on the plot. Fox was playing a business tycoon, Daniel Post, who hires the fictional law firm of Crane, Poole and Schmidt to defend him. Post had been sued for corrupting a clinical study for a new cancer-fighting drug by using his insider clout to ensure he was given the non-placebo. Interesting story line, but not helpful in the current reality.

Cancer treatment is sort of a moving target—things are always changing, and hopefully, improving. The cancer center has computers available for its patients, so we can check on the latest treatment, or clinical trial, available for our particular type of cancer.

The Melanoma Center at the University of California at San Francisco (UCSF) is world renowned. I could certainly transfer my case there, and surely be eligible for a number of clinical studies. Already two of my friends who live on the peninsula are readying their guest rooms for me, assuming that I will have to take up residence nearby for my treatment.

I'm lucky to have not only my medical oncologist looking into applicable trials, but an award-winning dermatologist, as well. She is also a friend, neighbor and the wife of our local city councilman, so she has been working hard on my case since she first heard my diagnosis.

She kept a steady stream of e-mails going to UCSF, checking on clinical trials, and getting second opinions on my course of treatment.

The standard treatment for malignant melanoma is Interferon—immunotherapy, rather than chemotherapy. Melanoma generally doesn't respond to chemotherapy drugs, so the body's natural immune system has to be beefed up to fight the onslaught of the melanoma cells.

In some recent cases, there have been clinical trials for melanoma that use other treatments, made from the patient's own blood cells. The obvious advantage of this option is that the awful side effects of Interferon can be avoided. But the results have not shown any more promise than the results from the standard use of Interferon.

My mother's friend didn't like the 50% or more chance of recurrence (in five years) that he was given, so when he learned (through the *cancer.gov* website sponsored by the National Institute of Health) about a trial study, he applied and was accepted. They used blood tests to find <u>which</u> type of melanoma he had. Then they took dendritic cells out of the blood, incubated with proteins from his type of melanoma and put them back in. After about nine months or a year a large dark mole on his forehead whitened, which indicated that the melanin was being attacked, and he's now past the five years with no recurrence. He gets follow-up tests with a dermatologist every three months and with the study people every six months.

My oncologist, even as he reviews with me the clinical trials he's aware of, thinks that my best bet is to stay put, and take the standard regimen.

In the end, it was confirmed by several other doctors that the standard course of Interferon was still the best bet.

So I won't be a guinea pig this time around.

Who knows what lies ahead.

15. Wish Upon a Star

I think the thing that I've found to be the most challenging about the cancer journey is that the road isn't straight. Often, when other kinds of medical challenges are put in our path, they are dealt with outright, and then recovered from directly. The line on the graph is more like a Bell curve: it goes up, then down. No matter how long each phase takes, it still follows the same basic pattern. Like appendicitis or a broken leg—you fix it, and then start on the road to recovery.

Cancer's a lot trickier than that. You're never quite sure when it's coming back, or where. The line on the graph is more like a wave, with lots of crests and valleys.

In my own journey, the first year was marked by an up-and-down series of events, starting with a series of biopsies, then surgery, followed by high-dose Interferon infusions, radiation treatments, and ½-dose Interferon home injections. It seems like 90% of what I'm fighting off is man-made medicine! My physical well-being jumped up and down depending on which treatment I was receiving. In the short periods in between, I might have felt and looked good, but I felt like it was deceptive and confusing to my friends, since I knew a week later I'd be laid low by the next round of treatments. I became apologetic when I was feeling good.

"You look great," says a friend.

"Don't look too close," I respond.

When it became clear that I would spend a year of my life on the side-effect-inducing Interferon, I took time to grieve for that year: for the loss of activity and productivity that I would surely face.

The first week of treatments alone would wipe out my attendance in five holiday luncheons around the state—the highlight of the year in my work with an association of retired clergy. (The hosts of each of those events got a cell phone call from the chemo ward instead.)

Having to sit in a chair for hours at a time with a tube stuck in your body is proportionately more difficult the more vibrant, youthful and active you are in your "regular" life. I like to think I still have some claim to those three categories.

I decided that before I entered that daily regimen, a little "R & R" would be in order.

"Chuck Myer! You have to spend a year on Interferon. What are you going to do?"

"I'm going to Disneyland!"

Ironically, months before, we had promised the kids we'd go to the 50th anniversary celebrations in Anaheim. We even bought tickets. But all that had been put on hold after my diagnosis and surgery.

When it became clear that I was recovering well from the major surgery in October (and three subsequent minor surgeries by the dermatologist), I checked with my oncologist about traveling to the Magic Kingdom over the Thanksgiving break. Not only did he approve it, he planned to go there the same week!

This turned out to be a great idea—it gave my family members a much needed break, and afforded a celebration of sorts, since it was looking like I was on the road to recovery (however long) as opposed to the other one.

We spent five days in "the happiest place on earth." Though I was trying to keep my mind off my medical dilemma, as I walked around the famous theme park I couldn't help noticing all of the young men who have shaved their heads and were out in the sun without a hat.

Being the new ambassador of skin cancer, I now walk up to total strangers and gently warn them about melanoma—encouraging them to use sun screen and/or hats... then I show them the scars on my head.

I saw one of those men again the next day, and he smiled and showed me his new hat.

I'm too old for the "Make-A-Wish" Foundation, but that didn't stop me from arranging my own magic wish. On Disneyland's Main Street USA, I got to stand and sing 4-part barbershop harmony with the "Dapper Dans" barbershop quartet, serenading members of my extended family who had joined us on our last day there.

The song?

"When You Wish Upon a Star."

Thanks, Walt, I needed that.

16. View from the Chemo Ward

It sucks to be me right now.

I'm sitting in a chair in the chemo center, with a drip line coming into the back of my hand, and I'm going to be here for a while.

OK, this is hard. And I'm going to have to do this every day.

The sportswriter Red Smith once said that being a writer is easy: you just sit down and open a vein. Well that's an appropriate analogy, I guess, since I'm doing both—figuratively and literally.

Every day I will spend at least three hours here. Once I get a chair (sometimes there's a wait), I get hooked up via a needle stick and a PIC (Percutaneous Intravenous Catheter) line, and start out with an hour's dosage of saline solution for general purposes. Then I get a blast of Kytril for anti-nausea protection. After that I get a bag of Benadryl to ward off chills and shakes. It also will make me sleepy. Finally I get the grand finale: Intron-A, the Interferon, which takes about 35 minutes to infuse into my system.

Some patients immediately start getting *rigor* (that's *rigor mortis* without dying). I will find that in my case, the side effects are delayed until after I get home.

This phase of treatment is four weeks in duration—or should I say enduration.

Due to some sort of twisted irony, my four weeks fall exactly between Thanksgiving and Christmas. Happy Holidays.

The thickness of the original tumor requires that I spend

almost all of the next year on Interferon. Starting in January, I will continue the Interferon treatments through self-injection at home. What will I be like after a year?

Day 1 is November 28. Before I go for my first Interferon infusion, I feel a need to test the baseline, because they say I am going to change. So I'm taking note of who I am, or at least who I am today.

I feel OK today. I am myself. I'm in a relatively good mood. I listen to some classical music, and some show tunes by Andrew Lloyd Webber.

I rake leaves. I address Christmas cards.

Then I go to the Cancer Center.

Will I change? How soon?

There are all kinds of warnings about depression as a result of taking Interferon. You even "need to have your head examined" before you take Interferon. So I endured an MRI—in an even tighter environment than the PET scan—in order to prove myself worthy of the treatment to come. Did I pass? I guess so.

Rather than end up on anti-depressants, I have obtained some joke books for my 11-year-old son, with instructions to keep me laughing when I come home from treatments. Actually, he could probably do that without the joke books—he's a funny guy.

There are others in the treatment room, all with their different concoctions of chemo drugs, shots, etc. Some are waiflike shadows of their former selves, some are young and vital. I know I'm subconsciously trying to find a chair near the second group.

I feel like my life has been hijacked. I have to be here every day. If I'm not here, I'm trying to get here, trying to get back, or trying to recover from what happened here.

Chuck Myer

It might even be easier if this was a depressing place, with Nazi-like nurses strapping you into metal-backed chairs under a single bare light bulb hanging from the ceiling. But no. The nurses are all magnificent. The room is beautiful, with right-angle picture windows framing a gorgeous view of no less a historic spot than Sutter's Fort itself. They change the seasonal, uplifting decorations regularly, and the chairs are all plush, adjustable lounge chairs. They're quite comfortable.

All of my doctors agree this is the best course of action, and that there are no clinical studies or trials that would be beneficial in my case. The infusion process takes up most of the afternoon, and the side effects kick in in the evenings.

Sure enough, the first two evenings found me squirming in bed with shakes, chills, aches and pains, and soreness in my surgical spots, followed by a huge spike in body temperature. Not a pretty picture.

That week they adjusted my anti-nausea meds, so that vomiting hasn't been a problem, and they started adding Benadryl, which decreased the other side effects significantly. So it seems the worst of it is over. I continue on this regimen until Christmas, and then go to 11 months of home self-injections at a lower dosage.

In the first month I can expect many of the possible side-effects of Interferon: rigor, fever and chills, shakes, tenderness at the site of my surgeries, mouth sores, fatigue, nausea, vomiting, loss of appetite, depression, etc. Basically I am going to feel like I have the flu for a year.

Every side effect leads to another prescription. Benadryl and Tylenol for the rigor and the shakes. Adavan for loss of sleep. Miles Mixture #10 for mouth sores. Colace for the constipation. (That got ugly.) Compazine for the nausea. Stannous fluoride to restore dental protection. Potassium for tiredness. Iron for anemia.

In the 11-month period I'll be checked for depression, thyroid problems and hair loss.

At home, I have to beg the pardon of my family members when the *rigor* shaking kicks in. They get used to seeing me "go to my room" to endure the chills under quilts and covers. (How appropriate that the cancer center had a quilt auction the same month.)

At home, I have to make the transition from patient lover to loving patient.

After twelve needle sticks in my left hand, the nurses tell me the veins won't take much more abuse. So I have to leave the needle, IV and PIC line in my wrist overnight. That means covering it with a glove and Saran Wrap if I want to shower or bathe.

I'm "draggin' wagon" near the end, although not as low as other Interferon patients usually are, according to the nurses and doctors.

Somehow I endure the four weeks, and on December 23 the heavy, daily treatments come to an end. The staff gives me a round of applause as I take a last look at the ecumenical decorations hanging throughout the facility. Happy Chanukah.

Merry Christmas.

17. The Cancer Club

I am getting a flood of get-well cards. I didn't quite expect that.

One cancer patient-friend told me to tape them all up on the wall so I could see them every day—that's what got her through. I haven't done that, although I'm sure that it worked magic for her.

Some people have sent me more than one card. Three, four, five, six. More often than not, the multiple senders are cancer survivors themselves. They are the ones who know it's not a one-time thing. It stays with you, and the road to recovery is long and lonely.

Clearly, some of the most sympathetic reactions I get are those from other cancer survivors and their families. They often seem to have the goal of recovery in focus, and are full of good advice. There is a whole network of them out there, sometimes almost working underground, it seems.

It's called the Cancer Club. And I'm a member now.

Did you know it was a club? I didn't.

These are the survivors, not the victims. These are the folks who want to talk turkey, not platitudes. They welcome me into their circle. They want details—they want to know about my blood counts, my markers, my staging. They aren't wringing their hands in desperation; they are putting their arm around me and trying to tell me how to beat this thing, what I should be doing, and what I shouldn't.

I knew I had become a card-carrying member when a big basket showed up at my front doorstep. Standing out on top was a baseball cap that read "Survivor." Inside was a set of survivor tools in a gift basket specifically designed for men with cancer. Inspired by cyclist Lance Armstrong's battle with testicular cancer, the basket contains his autobiography, an authentic "Livestrong" wristband, the Susie Mantell healing CD, 30 inspirational quotes on pop-open window cards, and a "Survivor" notebook and pen set (which is coming in handy right now). The basket even contained lip balm to soothe dry lips caused by stress and treatments, and peppermint tea, which really helps with nausea. There was a coffee mug: "I didn't survive cancer to die of stress!" I guess it replaced my mug with the big "C", which used to stand for Chuck.

I also got some subscriptions to magazines with names like "Coping" and "Cure," linking me with "club members" around the country.

But at times the "Cancer Club" can be as exclusive as a country club in Georgia.

It's difficult to describe, but people sharing various diseases now seem to form not only support groups, but cliques—and those can get pretty parochial. There is even jealousy sprouting up between the various support networks.

When Dick Clark made a TV appearance on New Year's Eve 2005/06 after suffering a stroke, it was pointed out how the struggles of stroke survivors are often overshadowed by the glare of the spotlight on cardiac and cancer survivors. And there are battle lines being drawn within the cancer community, as well.

For centuries, cancer was a word unspoken, an embarrassment suffered in silence. As if to annihilate that old paradigm, a lot of cancer survivors now wear their survivorship on their sleeves (or hats and T-shirts) as a proud badge of courage. The poster child for this new trend is the Susan G. Komen Foundation for Breast Cancer Research. The Komen Foundation is known for splashy events at which breast cancer survivors, dressed in pink, are heralded as heroes in the fight against pencil-pushing legislators and bureaucrats who haven't earmarked enough money for a "cure."

Breast cancer is big business. It's sexy. How could it fail? People like breasts. They come in very popular shapes and sizes.

But it's a little harder to get worked up about lung cancer.

A recent documentary on non-smoking women who have lung cancer showed the depth of the hard feelings. Their case is especially poignant, because the average person subconsciously blames lung cancer sufferers for their plight, since they assume it was brought on by smoking. Of course, quite often it is. It's easy to see that the poor wives of chain smokers who had to endure the second-hand smoke and now the disease might certainly feel some sense of injustice. But no one is marching in the streets for them—the breast parade is out there hogging up the whole boulevard.

There are even factions within the breast cancer community. Komen supporters are focused on the "cure," but not all medical professionals think that's the healthiest approach. The American Cancer Society and other organizations would have us look at prevention, as well. Though the causes of breast cancer aren't as clear as, say, lung cancer, it's quite possible that healthier diets, exercise and stress reduction might lower cancer diagnoses. It may be more complicated than, "the cure is there, we want it now, give us the money."

I appreciate the needs of each group, and I try to be supportive without taking sides. I have previously participated in the

Komen "Race for the Cure," and I'm currently rehearsing with "Sing for the Cure" (I am very thankful that the surgery on my neck hasn't impacted my vocal cords.)

I have joined several support groups to surround myself with survivors and to learn the tricks of their trade. There are support groups that focus on spirituality (even getting into comparative religions). There are support groups that encourage certain diets and other regimens. There are support groups that involve dance and movement therapy. There are support groups for the caregivers, as well.

For me, the most interesting of the groups meeting at the Sutter Cancer Center is the "Sutterwriters" group for cancer survivors, caregivers and health care workers. This group uses creative writing as a therapeutic tool. Members write quickly for 5-minute intervals to get out their feelings on various personal subjects, and then share their writings with others in the group. (The ground rules require positive feedback only.)

So being a member of the club has its rewards. Even a club where every single member would rather not be one.

18. Spiderman

To get to Oncology, Surgery and Chemotherapy, you go up in the cancer center elevator. But to get to Radiation, you have to go down. In a special elevator. Underground. Down. Into the dungeon.

That in itself should be ample warning.

From the very beginning, the staff "down below" struck me as different. The doctors seem to have their heads on straight. But some of their staff members have worked underground too long, I fear. They have weird demeanors and strange senses of humor.

I was informed that the first day of radiation treatment would be just with the technicians, and would be a "simulation." This session was designed as a dry run of my radiological treatment, in order for me to be properly "fitted."

Now I've had to adopt the personae of several superheroes in this endeavor already. I have felt like Superman and I've felt like the Incredible Hulk. Now, to prepare for radiation, I get to be Spiderman.

For the radiation beam, I have to have a tight, webbed "Spiderman" mask stretched over my head and face. It conforms to the contours of my head, and then dries into place. In a way, it seems like the next step in the natural progression of tight, enclosed spaces over my head, since I had previously gone into the restrictive circular PET-CAT scanner, and then later into the more claustrophobic MRI mask. This just brought it all full circle, I guess.

The webbed blue mask is designed to secure my head and

Melanoma Melodrama

keep me strapped down in just the right position each time I'm about to get my "hypofractional" (translation: infrequent, large) dose of radiation.

The other part of my superhero personae was my first tattoo! And my second, third and fourth. These were injected as part of the effort to delineate the exact places on my body that will receive radiation. The tattoos are made in the usual way, and are permanent, but are small enough to be insignificant in the larger view of things. (My dermatologist, who is now on guard for any unusual spots on my skin, noticed them right away, though no one else has.)

Like some of their counterparts in the floors above ground, the medical technicians in radiology have a little trouble relating to the patient as a human. (I suppose this is understandable when a person's face has been masked off with thick blue mesh.)

So my body is lying in the center of the room, and they seem to approach it more as a problem to be solved. I caught a couple of them coming into the room and discussing my case as if I wasn't there.

"How do you do?" I said. "I'm Chuck Myer."

Most of the patients don't try to talk, instead preferring to "zone out." When the writer Anais Nin went through radiation, she tried to block out reality and visualize the most beautiful scenes from her life as she underwent the treatment. I had used similar techniques when I was stuck for longer periods of time in the MRI unit.

So the radiology staff gave me the four tattoos and made measurements and calculations that will help them during the radiation treatments.

At one point, I was sequestered under my blue mask while

technicians hovered over my neck, working on the markings they use for the equipment. One was having trouble with the ink solution.

"Do you want some alcohol?" asked her co-worker.

From beneath the mask comes my voice: "No, thanks, I'm fine."

* * * *

The plan is that I would receive five treatments on my neck (the lymph node surgery area) in the month of January. The actual treatments would only take at most about 15 minutes, two times a week.

But there is some eerie communication disconnect between the doctors and the technicians. (On one occasion, the mousiest of these underground mice led me back to see the doctor, weighed me in, and put me in a consultation room to wait. Five minutes later she comes back to announce: "The doctor isn't here today.")

I had to insist to see a doctor, because the technicians had even started to set up the procedures before I had actually been told exactly which sites were going to be radiated. The original paperwork they were using showed that both my head and neck would be radiated. But I never got a chance to talk to the radiology oncologist after the pathology report came back with the welcome news that no cancer cells were found at the incision on my head. So I maintained that my head didn't need to be radiated, just my neck.

What would I risk by having my head radiated? Well, frying my brain is a consideration. Radiating your head isn't something you want to do if there is no benefit (a fact to bear in mind 2 years later). Also, I would have lost my hair. Not that that would necessarily be a "deal-killer." But since the chances of

Melanoma Melodrama

any cancer at the original site were extremely low, why lose the hair?

The doctor eventually agreed with me, so it was a good thing I had specifically asked for a chat with him. So we proceeded with the neck alone as the radiation site. This is where the infected node was removed, so presumably the radiation would help kill any infections in other nodes or in the "surgical bed" where the first "sentinel" node was removed. The pathology report also showed no further evidence of cancer in my neck, but the radiologists say there's a 40% chance of recurrence there, and radiating could cut that to a third of the chance. They will try to avoid radiating my taste buds (which are already compromised by Interferon).

Everything sees to be odds-making at this level. My medical oncologist had put the chances at 30-40%. I wonder what odds Jimmy the Greek would give me?

I sought out a second and third opinion, and I was impressed by the knowledge and explanatory skills of the radiation doctors. They told me about the pioneering work done at MD Anderson Cancer Center in Houston, where the high dose regimen for radiating melanoma was developed.

The five dosages passed quickly without further incident, and after the final treatment, the black receptionist in the basement told me I should do "the happy dance." (I did.) She even offered to sing "Pomp and Circumstance"—and sure enough, they even gave me a diploma. And a trophy: I get to keep my mask.

What I didn't quite realize at first, though, is that the aftereffects of the radiation don't end when the treatments do. In fact, they often don't even start until a couple of weeks later. So when my neck started feeling tight and hot and later blistery, I

Chuck Myer

wasn't quite sure what to make of it.

I feel fear when I think of the tiny vessels that drain from my head into my neck. Are there cancer cells still there, in hiding? What if they were "out swimming" somewhere between my head and neck on the day of the surgery?

Is it the radiation that causes my neck to blister and burn, or is it fear?

19. Inject Thyself

The last part of my treatment is the longest. Eleven months. I now take the Interferon at home—as an injection that I have to administer myself, three nights a week.

So the routine breaks down into two parts. The first is the shots themselves, including the needles, the alcohol swabs, the "pens" with 60 million units of Interferon in each, the biohazard waste disposal bin I keep for the needles and the spent pens.

The needles themselves are so thin these days, they really do not cause pain if they're inserted correctly. I just have to learn to wash my hands thoroughly, and use alcohol swabs on the needle base (and on my skin). I test each needle before use, and rotate the dial to my dosage: 20 million units. My injections are done subcutaneously, which means they just go into the fat layer below the skin of my thigh or abdomen. I may be losing weight, but there's still plenty of flesh to get the job done.

I even had a friend, a cancer patient and retired nurse in her 70s, offer to give me the shots. Now that was a nice offer. But the sheer logistics of her getting her feeble body to my house three nights a week at my bedtime seemed totally ludicrous. Besides, after the first few injections, there was never any problem doing it myself. My wife didn't offer to do the injections, and only watched the process once. Still, I have no complaints on that score.

The medicine is very expensive; thousands of dollars. Even just the co-pay is $25 a week for a year. The Interferon has to stay refrigerated, so shipping and delivery are a logistical problem. So is any travel I try to do on Mondays, Wednesdays or

Fridays. And the needles and pens have to be deposited in a biohazard container. I'm becoming an expert. I'm even starting to understand the words on the pen from the doctor's office: *"Octreotide acetate for injectible suspension."*

The other half of the equation is the after-effects. That's a slightly different story. I take Tylenol PM when I have a shot, just like they gave me in the chemo ward when I had the infusions.

I've had all of the same side effects I had during infusions, just slightly less intense. Usually the day after the week's first injection is filled with the most fatigue, chills and headaches. Nausea follows on the next day. Then it's time for another shot.

The 11-month prescription is standard. The dose for melanoma patients doesn't ever vary the way it often does for people with other cancers. That's because there is no good way to track melanoma. So I have to take 144 injections because that's the way they did it in the clinical study some years ago—not based on any feedback data in my particular case. My oncologist even admits that any success from the full treatment could have been derived solely from the first month's infusions alone. In other words, the self-injections could easily be superfluous for all we know.

One of the biggest concerns is depression. The day after a dose of Interferon, a person is likely to stay in bed fighting off the side effects and feeling lousy, with no energy to face the day. These symptoms look a lot like clinical depression, and can lead to it if the patient is already pre-disposed in that direction. And one friend of mine summarized the futile spiral that can ensue:

"Yeah, I had melanoma," he says. "I lost all of the lymph nodes in my groin. They put me on Interferon but it made me depressed. So they gave me anti-depressants, but I got hooked on them."

I know where he's coming from. I get terribly frustrated by my own lack of productivity. The cancer medication is "interferin'" with my ability to focus, to concentrate on daily tasks and work projects. The medication causes nausea and chills, and often the only way to avoid the side effects is to sleep them off. So my days are sometimes filled with groggy sleep, punctuated by frustration when nothing seems to click; nothing seems to get accomplished. And just as the cycle ends, it begins again—it's time for another injection. Self-injection, ironically—I have to administer the dose myself.

How can you tell the difference between "real" clinical depression and Interferon-induced depression?

I guess I'll find out during the long haul…

20. That's Depressing

I thought I was going to make it. I thought I had settled into a routine with my Interferon injections. It was a long haul, but while certainly not pleasant, it was somehow bearable. I knew which days would bring on which challenges, and I knew how to prepare for them.

But then something changed. I was having trouble coping. When I still had six months to go, it seemed like forever. I was trying to keep up with all of my activities, responsibilities and hobbies. One of them, a weekly 3-hour evening music rehearsal with a barbershop chorus, required standing on risers. That was more than I could handle after an injection, so I slid my injection schedule over one day to accommodate. But the change in the weekly schedule had a residual effect on me and my other activities through the week.

Mostly it was an intensification of the fatigue I was already dealing with. It was "fatigue fatigue"—an inability to make it through the day, and a growing frustration with the increasing need to lie down several times in the middle of the day.

New side effects were now being added to the list, which grew to 15. Of the two worst new ones, sexual dysfunction and depression, I was a lot more worried about the latter. At least the sexual dysfunction could be assumed to be temporary. And my oncologist did prescribe Levitra, which was used with a modicum of success.

But when depression rears its ugly head, you never know how long it will stay. As the summer wore on, I found myself staying quiet and suffering through my day-time naps with guilt over my non-productivity. And once or twice I felt myself slipping below the "depression line," which I visualized with a sign reading, "Danger Zone."

As it turned out, these moments were during my spouse's extended absences, so I had been overcompensating as a single parent, and not getting the rest I desperately needed. So that turned out to be mercifully temporary. But the demons had been aroused, and had made their presence known.

I knew enough about depression to know that it can reach a stage where it becomes a clinical, medical condition. I was determined not to let this happen.

To make sure I had all the bases covered, I reported all of this to my oncologist. I certainly didn't want a prescription for depression—I was already juggling 14 prescriptions as it was.

So I went of my own volition to see a counselor who worked at the Cancer Center. This is certainly a great service to provide—and at no charge, just a donation. I spent the first hour with her, basically recapping my recovery program up to that point. I must have said all the right buzz words, because at the end of the time I'm sure she was convinced that I was in no real danger of a permanent problem (and I'm sure she has many patients who are in danger). So like all of the other "new" side effects, I proceeded under the assumption that all would be well in November, after that magical day when I would give myself the last injection.

Here, I think, is one of the true turning points, one of the keys to my success in recovery. I made the conscious decision that I would fight depression on my own, by focusing my spiritual, mental and emotional energies on the problem, rather than popping another pill to "solve" it.

I wonder how many doctors would have been more apt to

prescribe depression medication if I had been female? A book I had read, "Male Practice," by Robert Mendelsohn, made a strong case for exposing gender-based inequities along these lines.

At any rate, I identified what I felt was my worst day, isolated it, and labeled that as "rock bottom." Then I visualized coming back up from that point. I had accumulated "visualization" tapes and CDs for cancer patients, and I did use some of them, but I found that generating my own music and words, spoken and written, to be more helpful than those of others. Perhaps those tapes served to start my own creative juices rolling.

I looked at the calendar and counted the number of injections I had remaining. I measured out the number of needles and alcohol swabs that I would need, and returned the extras to the chemo ward.

The box of supplies now served as a count down calendar. As the box got emptier and emptier, my spirits rose.

I started making plans for my post-Interferon life, including activities which I couldn't have handled even as I was making the plans. One was a trip to New York to visit my daughter, by then a freshman at New York University.

The holidays were approaching, and one of my jobs requires a lot of travel in early December. (I hadn't been able to do that the previous December, which I spent in the chemo ward. While the Christmas season is supposed to be "filled with joy," I knew professionally that it was also a time when depression also flared, leading to higher rates of suicide and sudden death than other times in the year. So I built up my strength and defenses to fend off any problems in that area, resolving not to let the myriad holiday preparations feel oppressive and overwhelming.

As the magic date, November 15, approached, I made arrangements to celebrate the day, which would hopefully mark my return to "normal" society. I agreed to be a speaker at a monthly evening service at our church which coincidentally(?) would be held that same day (see next chapter, *Testimony*).

This visioning helped me turn the corner and continue to raise my spirits as the piles of needles and swabs got smaller and smaller, and eventually disappeared.

21. Testimony

Oral presentation - November 15, 2006
United Methodist Church of Rancho Cordova

Last night after the Dixie Chicks' concert, just after midnight, I went into the upstairs bathroom for the 150th time, took out the last needle in my little kit, and injected 20 MIUs (million international units) of the cancer drug Interferon into my body.

These shots carry some good news and bad news.

The good news: They make the needles very thin these days.

The bad news: There are side effects. Let me show the list of side effects that they put in the box. *(Here I unrolled a super-long instruction sheet.)*

I didn't suffer from all of them. There were some I managed to avoid. I only got about 14-15 of them. Here they are from north to south:

Headaches
Dizziness
Extreme fatigue
Depression
Xerostomia (dry mouth)
Pain in my surgical area
Asthma
Phlegm production
Reflux

Melanoma Melodrama

Chills and fever (rigor)
Nausea
Skin rash and infection
E.D. (if you don't know, don't ask)
Constipation (don't ask about that either)

What's worse is I have a pill or prescription for each of those side effects. You can imagine what my medicine cabinet looks like. Most of these side effects aren't visible to my friends and acquaintances, or even my family, even though I suffered from them daily. For the most part, "I looked fine."

(To person in the front row: "Don't I look fine?")

I figured I had to work through the side effects and continue with my daily life no matter how I felt. But watching me do productive things and participate in my normal activities made it look to others that "I was fine." I really wasn't.

The worst of the side effects were fatigue and depression. These two worked together to push me down in a dangerous spiral. On the average, I lost about half of each working day's productivity because I had to take a couple of 500-ml tablets of generic acetaminophen and lay down. Now I find out that wasn't even safe—that's the aspirin that just got recalled!

When you're like me, and you are in bed during the day, you start feeling guilty about what you're not doing that you're supposed to be doing. That starts the cycle of depression.

I know that I've been difficult to live with during this period, and if I was short-tempered with anyone during this time, I want to apologize. I take responsibility—I can't blame everything on the medication.

What I learned is this: now when I see someone who looks "fine," I will remember that he or she could be hurting inside, churning over with unseen problems. We all have to deal with pains and hurts that aren't obvious—I will always remember that.

But here comes the real good news: The shot I took last night was the last one. Yes! I have completed a year of Interferon treatment, and so I can hope for a more normal life.

Thus ends the most difficult year of my life. In case you're just meeting me tonight, let me recap: last September, doctors found a malignant melanoma on my scalp. It had already metastasized to the lymph nodes.

When some people get cancer, there is a tendency to start to ask "Why me?" and all of the "What ifs." This is especially true for unseen skin cancer on the back of the head. There really isn't any explanation for how I got it. It's not like the person who gets cancer and says "Why me?" and God's answer comes down from heaven: "Well, you did smoke cigarettes for thirty years. I put the little warning labels on every pack, didn't you see them?" I didn't have time to waste wondering why God was doing this to me. I don't see God as a being who is "up there" meting out punishment or pain. Melanoma is a natural phenomenon that seems to be increasing in occurrence, possibly related to global warming and other changes in the environment.

When I got the diagnosis, I got quickly to work scheduling medical procedures. In October 2005, I had more of my scalp removed, as well as 33 lymph nodes from my neck. After I had partially recovered, I was sent in to the chemo ward, where the first larger doses of Interferon were administered. I sat in the chemo chair every weekday between Thanksgiving and Christmas. I had radiation treatments starting in January 2006, which was also the month they trained me how to inject the Interferon into my body.

I still have to be checked out with a PET scan to see if all of the cancer is gone, but I remain very hopeful that that will come out with good news. Meanwhile, I want to thank my church family for all of their love and support during this difficult time.

My friend Julie Hughes is a singer/songwriter in the Bay Area, and when I first told her about my diagnosis, she said, "Is there anything I can do?" I immediately said, "Yes, you can write me a song." And so she did. This song is called, "My Battle Won," so it's perfect for tonight. I may not yet have won my battle over melanoma, but I have surely won the battle over Interferon.

Can't take away my guiding light
Can't take away all the joy in my life
Nothing can separate me from God's love
He's got me surrounded, my battle won!

22. Triumph

Gradually, cancer patients realize there are a few "bennies" out there—free, supportive programs for cancer patients provided by various foundations, charities, etc.

After the initial shock, I learned to enjoy having valet parking at the Sutter Cancer Center, and coffee when I got inside. I even got a free hat there also, to cover my scalp scars. Cancer patients wind up with a drawer full of free T-shirts from fundraisers and walk-a-thons. The UC Davis Cancer Center has a "Learn at Lunch" program where not only do they bring in expert speakers on cancer-related subjects, they provide the proverbial free lunch as well.

One of the best offers came my way at just the right time—right after I completed my dreadful year of Interferon treatments. I was constantly tired, I had lost a lot of weight, and my wife said my posture was poor.

So my ears perked up when a journalist friend told me about "Triumph." It's basically a strength-and-fitness program designed for cancer survivors.

I have never joined a weight-training gym, mostly because of the (perceived) expense. If I'm going to exercise, I always rationalized, why not just walk, jog or cycle for free in my neighborhood, or use some of the discarded, unused exercise equipment donated by church members.

But this program was free for cancer survivors, initially funded by a grant from the Lance Armstrong Foundation. So my economic rationale evaporated.

The local Triumph program had been set up by Pam White-

Whitehead, a Sacramento architect and cycling fan who had survived uterine cancer. Like many of us, Whitehead had been inspired by Armstrong and his battle back from metastasized cancer to cycling superstardom. It was her "legwork" that got the initial 2004 prize money—the $5,000 Lori A. Tilton Peloton Triumph Award—and she continues to serve as primary fundraiser for the Triumph program.

The program is a partnership between the medical staff and patient educators at UC Davis Cancer Center and 650 FIT, a contemporary fitness center off of Howe Avenue in Sacramento. For ten weeks, twice a week, cancer survivors in the program have full use of 650 FIT's extensive collection of weight-training and gym equipment.

So I signed on. We just had to show willingness to commit to the program and to notify our doctors of our actions. On the first day, we met the sponsors and each other, and took a test of our dexterity that was to be repeated on the last day to measure our improvement. We were told how the program was designed to reverse some of the debilitating effects of cancer and its treatment, and to help us lead fuller, healthier lives.

As we settled into the routine, we started each day with 15 minutes on the cardiovascular treadmills, stationary bicycles and elliptical machines. Then for 45 minutes we would move on to the many weightlifting machines that are purported to exercise each of the 650 muscles in the body. Our trim, 20-something trainers watched over us and helped us navigate all the controls and levers.

I did leg curls and extensions. I did chest presses. I did shoulder presses. I did leg presses. I did seated row exercises, calf raises, bicep curls and tricep curls.

Near the close of each session, we adjourned to the group

exercise room, where our two trainers led us in sit-ups and stretching exercises for our abs (whatever those are).

I certainly did gain strength during the ten weeks of the program, although I was bound to show a lot of improvement as my body recovered from the onslaught of Interferon. I was able to maintain my lower weight, and I could feel strength returning in terms of both muscle mass and cardiovascular endurance.

I fear these kinds of fitness centers are more often the setting for competitiveness and personal despair. But our group seemed devoid of the competitive drive—instead, we concentrated on competing only against our own goals and "personal bests."

I believe that women are much better at this than men. There's a pre-programmed evolutionary drive wired into the testosterone that causes men to want to compete or try to outdo each other. I had to learn to ignore the pumped-up he-men at the other stations who were stacking the 50-pound weights onto their machines while probably silently laughing at my puny weight stacks. It would have been easier if I could have just averted my eyes from one man's triangular frame and Velcro muscle belt. But the problem was aural as well—he had a personal trainer who continually barked out instructions, counts and militaristic commands as his client groaned and grunted under the huge weights. Seeing this guy and me in the same weight room reminded me of the political cartoons from the recent California gubernatorial campaign. There was quite a visual contrast between Phil Angelides, whose bespectacled visage could have been illustrated in the dictionary under "nerd," and Arnold Schwarzenegger, Mr. Olympia and star of "Pumping Iron" and countless action movies.

I had to remember that I was there for myself and to pursue

Melanoma Melodrama

my own goals. I was a cancer survivor, battling my way back to health, not someone trying to impress babes on the beach.

More important than the actual body-building aspect was the built-in support network the program almost guaranteed. My fellow "Triumphians," 75% of whom were female, were in all the different stages of treatment, recovery and recurrence, so we provided support and encouragement to each other as appropriate. One woman in the group had been diagnosed with, and recovered from, melanoma before I was born! Now that's the kind of story that gives someone like me real encouragement.

We naturally shared our own cancer stories with each other as we treaded, lifted and stretched. It's often easier to talk to other cancer patients, because they "know the lingo" and you don't have to tread lightly the way you do with friends and healthy strangers. We shared information about other similar programs, and even attended other events together.

The majority of those in the program were like me—battling back. But a few were still in active treatment, and more than one received bad news from medical tests during the ten weeks. I felt bad sharing my own good results from medical tests while those of some of my friends were going the other way.

One woman in the group shared my penchant for "self-journalism." But while I was carrying a pen and paper, she was carrying a tape recorder. Already an accomplished radio journalist, she found it natural to record not only her own reactions along the cancer trail, but those of her doctors and caregivers as well. The sound of the voices of medical personnel as they deliver cancer test results is not something you can bind into a book. She had had a number of programs broadcast on local radio and, remarkably, I had heard one of them just before I met her on the first day of class. She and I also shared concern, as parents, for ways to ease the impact on our school-age children.

Our culminating week included "closure" with our sponsors, a group photograph, and a re-test with the exercise balls and balance exercises. My tests showed excellent improvement.

As a symbol of our joint achievement, some of us participated in a 5-kilometer walk/run on an early Sunday morning that same week. The event, called "Shamrock'n," also included a half-marathon option, which our 650 FIT trainers did while we survivors walked the 5K. It was fun to cheer on our trainers as they whizzed by in the spots where the two courses coincided.

As for our group of survivors, rather than each going at our own speed, we opted to walk together (at the speed of "the slowest ship in the convoy") and cross the finish line together. Over 1,000 others crossed the finish line before we did. But we didn't care. We had made it.

In reaching our own personal goals, we had each "triumphed" in first place.

And I got another T-shirt to add to the drawer-full!

23. No Scintigraphic Evidence

Time to make an appointment at my friendly "imaging center" to get another PET scan. (It still gives me shivers to walk into a building labeled "Nuclear Medicine.")

PET stands for Positron Emission Tomography, a high-tech computerized camera that uses scintigraphic imagery (radioactivity) to miraculously find a cancer, stage it, and show whether it has spread to other parts of the body.

But it's not an easy procedure.

What's the scariest thing I have found about getting a PET scan?

Is it the grueling regimen the day before, when they make you OD on proteins and avoid all carbs the day before, and then make you fast for a day?

Is it the process of having radioactive fluids injected into your bloodstream until you yourself become radioactive?

Is it the thought of having your arms strapped to your sides and being tied onto a conveyor belt and sent into a tube—with no clear idea how long you'll have to remain motionless, unable to even scratch your nose?

For me, after going through the process four times, it was none of these things.

It was the music.

When they give you the radioactive injection, it takes up to an hour for it to go through the bloodstream. So you have to sit still. No problem, I thought. I always carry a book.

But no. They don't let you read! Reading, explained the nuclear nurse, is "active." She wants to keep me "passive."

Right. She says reading gets the sucrose juices flowing. In the wrong direction, evidently. Perhaps it depends on what you're reading?

Instead they want you to sit motionless in the chair for about an hour. All you can do is listen to music. But their music is a piped-in collection of rejected popular tunes from the 1950s! Usually when you're listening to music you always have the ("active") ability to change the channel. But when you're passively motionless, you have to take it as it comes. Here you're held hostage listening to "Chances Are," "Red Roses for a Blue Lady" and "Smoke Gets in Your Eyes."

Ouch!

Like so many prisoners of war before me, I had to invent mental exercises and gyrations to keep myself sane. I tried concentrating on memorizing the playlist—so I could describe to others the torture I endured. I tried listening only to the musical accompaniment, visualizing the printed musical score as the notes and musical directions floated by in real time—as if I was conducting the orchestra. I even tried predicting what the next song would be!

Nothing worked. When the nurse finally returned, I blurted out, "I'll confess! I'll name names! Just make it stop!"

Note to self: Next time, bring an IPOD.

* * * *

After the day of the test, you get to endure the long wait for results. Many cancer patients find this to be the most agonizing thing about the process. They sit by the phone biting their fingernails for days at a time.

Well, I don't. I have invented a slightly twisted mental exercise that gets me through it.

OK, bear with me on this. This is how I rationalize the wait for results of a cancer test.

First of all, I don't agonize over whether the results are going to be good or bad. I look at it this way: if there is a problem, it's already there, and the test is just going to identify it. Knowledge is power. The more information I have about what is going on in my body, the better. And if there isn't a problem, all the better.

OK, so we've established that "all test results are good." So how to handle delays and even miscommunications? Well, this harkens back to how we anticipate anything good in our lives—be it dessert, a romantic interlude, a chocolate truffle, a check in the mail. Some people have to have instant gratification. Others have learned to enjoy the anticipation. I'm in the second group.

I know others who are always looking for immediate gratification. My theory here is simple: people who are raised in large families learn to grab the goodies quick, or there won't be anything left. Only children or those in small families, like me, didn't have that problem growing up. So I can wait.

The wait was a long one in February 2007 when my third PET scan was done to measure the effectiveness of my year of Interferon treatments. The test results were misplaced and not sent to all of the oncologists. With me in his office nine days later, Dr. Ow had to phone "Nuclear Medicine" to have them fax over the results. But they weren't disappointing:

02/07/07:

"Negative PET scan showing no scintigraphic evidence of recurrent or metastatic malignant melanoma."

Sounds good to me.

24. Randomness and Religion

Since my cancer diagnosis at age 51, I've calculated the amount of time I've spent ruminating on the following questions:

Why me?

Why did God choose to smite me with cancer?

Is it something I did? Or said?

Am I being punished for my own sins, or the "sins of the fathers"?

Do I need to pray for forgiveness before I can pray for healing?

I've faithfully attended church all of my life—why didn't that protect me from this?

Does God have some purpose in choosing to give me melanoma, and have it sneak up on me like that—on the back of my head where I couldn't see it?

What bargain must I strike to be cured?

As I said, I've totaled up the amount of time I've spent thinking about these questions.

It's zero.

That probably would have been different if this had happened to me in an earlier phase of my life. I have traveled a long way in my own faith journey, starting out as a prize-winning Sunday School pupil. Most of those Sunday School teachers in the 50s and 60s would have said that the questions I listed above were exactly the right questions to ask, and they would have supplied me with the "correct" answers, as well.

I went along with that program as a child. As a teenager, I

did not rebel; I tried to do what was expected of me. I remember reading a student editorial about God in an alternative student magazine at my high school. It read, in part, "What is God?... God is certainly not a wise, bearded old man sitting on his throne in heaven."

My reaction at the time: "He's not??"

And with that question, my questioning began, and eventually flowered and matured. It was a process that took decades. It took a lot of dialogue. It took a lot of reading from the pens of many great thinkers… even those who wrote the Bible. It took a lot of reflection. And it took a lot of work to reopen parts of my mind that had been prematurely roped off in childhood.

The force that created the sun as well as my errant skin cells, and the ensuing tumor, is not a human force. It cannot be shoehorned into a box full of personifications of human emotions. The list of questions I began with is full of such personifications: choosing, smiting, punishing, forgiving, bargaining.

God is essentially a human construct. In fact, humans have constructed quite a wide variety of gods. We've been building these constructs as best we can, since we've been able to reason in order to explain our place here. But all of our constructs will fall short.

So my cancer is another in a series of billions of seemingly random events. It puts me in my place to realize that there is no Oz-like "creator of the universe," up there calculating the pros and cons of keeping Chuck Myer on earth. Instead, I am delightfully part of a remarkably random universe.

What I choose to do about staying in it, however, is anything but random.

25. Italy

We were flying over the Alps. Fifty of us—on an adventure of a lifetime. We were heading for Malpensa Airport in Milan, the beginning of a ten-day tour among the top locations of Italy for art and architecture, including Milan, Sirmione, Verona, Venice, Pisa, Montecatini, Florence, Assisi, Rome and the Vatican City.

The spiritual leader of this trek was Bishop Beverly Shamana of the United Methodist Church from Northern California and Nevada. Bishop Shamana had been in office since 2000, and was nearing the conclusion of her eight-year term, with retirement looking good to her now, less than a year away. Most bishops and pastors take groups to the Holy Land, or along Paul's journeys in the Middle East. Italy, it would seem, has nothing for United Methodists, since it is well over 90% Catholic. But Bishop Shamana, a world-renowned gourd artist and former music teacher, was intensely interested in the Renaissance. So she worked with *Educational Opportunities* in Florida to come up with their first tour of the art and architecture of Italy.

I served as an assistant tour guide promoting the trip, having worked for the Church in journalistic and administrative lay roles. I was also the head of Sacramento's art docents, leading tours of public art (and sometimes architecture) downtown, and training others how to do so.

And I had lived most of the past year free from Interferon, free from cancer, and free to pursue my life without the worries of 2005-06. I was ready for some travel!

Melanoma Melodrama

The majority of the group, lay people in their 60s and 70s, and mostly women, hadn't met me before, but we set off for Italy anticipating the many things we would see.

During the nine-hour flight from Atlanta to Malpensa, I was glad my seat-mate spoke only Italian, so I didn't have to talk.

Soon after we arrived, we visited perhaps the only Methodist Church in Italy. It was a struggling little place in Milan, led by David and Kristin Markay, an energetic pastor couple. As a journalist, I was ready with the pad and pencil and camera, to get the story. The communications director would be waiting in California as I "wired" the story and photos back home.

On my pad, I had some trouble getting his name.

A bit jet-lagged from the plane trip, I found some of the church literature, and that took care of it.

Or did it?

That was it for religion; now it was on to the great art. And I appreciated it all. Each place we went, I went farther, often setting off alone on our breaks, traveling away from the heavy tourist areas and seeing farther beyond what the shop owners would have us see. It was marvelous.

Meanwhile, each day, my roommate Bruce and I were expected to be sending in the photos and stories. But when my camera battery needed recharging, I couldn't do it. I had brought the appropriate charger and European converter, but I couldn't make it happen.

The hotels had computers for the American traveler, but each keyboard was different! The "@" sign was never on "2"—it was always someplace different.

My mind was having a hard time handling these tricky little mechanical details.

Still, my body, now fortified by the "Triumph" program, was having a great time. In Sirmione and Verona, I started doing some major walking. In Venice, during our break, I chose to walk through six of the existing *sestieres* (sub-cities) beyond the one where Venice tourists stay. I invited an old friend, Myrtle Findley, for that walk. She was happy to come with me, and we shared a nice lunch in the Campo del Bartolomeo. We covered a lot of ground, and I only made a few mistakes. Myrtle enjoyed the outing, realizing she alone never would have traveled as far as we did. When we returned, it was time for the "required" gondola ride.

It reminded me of my trips to Europe in college—taking off with a map, assuming I knew the way despite major differences in not only map-making but city-making.

The next day we were headed for Pisa; I was looking forward to seeing the Leaning Tower. But first, it was my day to lead the meditation. I had flyers for everyone. We would close with "Leaning on the Everlasting Arms."

But I just couldn't say it. Try as I might, I couldn't finish my sentences. Somehow I finished off the presentation. Most of the people, who didn't really know me, didn't realize it was short on my end. Still, somehow I knew from that point, I

Melanoma Melodrama

wouldn't be speaking in long sentences on this trip.

It was starting. Something in my brain was awry; I knew it was there, but I didn't know what to do about it . . .

Meanwhile, my body was raring to go. Our tour guide, Lorna, told us that after many years of remodeling, tourists were now able not only to go in, but could go up to the top— if they had a 15-euro ticket, and several hours to wait. She asked if any of us wanted to go in, and if so, to go right to the ticket counter. I did.

There was one ticket for 4:00 p.m. But that's when we needed to board for the hotel. There was no way. I talked to them in my brief Italian (I had just taken a few classes)—but no deal. I still wanted to go. I found Lorna and had her talk to the ticket agents. And boy, was she good. She went in there blasting away, and sure enough, came out with one ticket for 3:00. I went over about 2:00, just to make sure I was first in line.

At 3:00, the rope was lifted, and I was on my way. There were 294 steps in the circular stairway —each one of them different, from all the feet that have indented the centers of them over 800 years.

There were others there, younger than me, who couldn't make it—I tried to help them. There were breaks along the way, as others came down, but it wasn't long before I made it to the top landing of the Leaning Tower of Pisa. This is where Galileo did his experiments on gravity!

Just then I saw, still above me, a ladder up to the top of the bells above me. I couldn't let that pass—and soon I was above the bells, looking down on the amazing Italian landscape before me!

I wrote up the article about the trip. It sounded like a watershed moment from me, rather than the group. I sent it anyway, and it went out on the Internet.

I was buying one-time use cameras now, and taking what shots I could. The computer at Montecatini still had strange keyboard info, but at least it was free (not like the one in Venice, which also suffered breakdowns).

The next day was Florence. I enjoyed seeing Michelangelo's David, first from its original outdoor site (where a duplicate now stands) and then the original in the Galleria dell'Accademia, along with many other Renaissance sculptures of Michelangelo and the masters.

That afternoon was free time—and I took off: first across the Arno into Pilazzo Pitti, then back through the Via del Terme and the Via del Tornabuoni, where I visited a church and a faire, all beyond the usual tourist spots.

I was walking alone in a pleasant neighborhood, when someone recognized me as an American from the back: by the stitching of the trademark name on my backpack! He was American, too, with a gentle Southern twang. He didn't want to seem rude, but I was easily befriended. I spoke to him as much as I could, and learned he had friends in small towns in California where I had worked and lived. We got to his hotel and said good-bye.

I could somehow tell that my speech was better with strangers.

I walked back down to the Piazza della Signoria and to the bus.

The next day, we headed for Rome, with a major stop in Assisi. Poor Assisi, hardly anyone spends the night there, but they have a lot of day-trippers. For my roommate and fellow journalist, Bruce, this was the highlight of the trip. He did the meditation, and I wrote it up. The basilica, named for St. Francis, kept going down: three huge floors down until the relics of St. Francis were before us.

Again, I enjoyed walking through the medieval streets, alone.

Soon we were in Rome, the final destination (for those of us who were not taking the travel extension to Sorrento). Everything in Rome came together in a complete circle—centuries and centuries of art in huge museums, often sitting on top of other buildings at lower layers of soil: the churches and monuments of the past. We have no idea what it's like to live in a place with that much "historicity."

I got lost in the Vatican, when I went to buy another camera—in fact, that might have happened anyway, and the group itself got lost among the huge hordes inside. I was so happy to find them in the Sistine Chapel, I almost forgot to look up!

In the Colosseo the next day, I just savored the inside and took everything in. I knew I'd be heading for home the next day; this was the grand finale. We toured to the Foro Romano, with a crazy tour guide. We walked through downtown Rome, ending up at the Trevi Fountain (the tourist area "headquarters"). Again, we were given one last "free time" out.

I was on one last mission: to find the "Santa Teresa in Ecstasy" statue by Bernini, featured in Dan Brown's "Angels and Demons." It was at a church many blocks away. By now I knew that most churches weren't open at 2:00 – the national siesta. But I didn't care. I just wanted to find it. I took off walking.

I walked and walked, leaving the tourists way behind. Despite the maps, strange street signals, and Dan Brown's errors, I found it. Locked, of course. But I put my name and address into a mail slot in the door. Perhaps I was begging Santa Teresa to help me.

Chuck Myer

The melanoma was back, and I didn't even realize it. It had been creeping into my brain for weeks now, and yet the little indications didn't reveal it. It had sequestered a spot in my head where it would morph into a silent 5-6 centimeter tumor, leaving, for now, only my speech a little slurred.

I made it back to the Trevi Fountain, and we took one more walk to the Pantheon and Piazza Navona. We were done now, and my job almost completed. At night, I was on the computer one more time—not to file a story. I was letting my doctor know that I was coming in.

Early the next morning, we took off in the bus in the dark before breakfast. It would be the longest day of my life.

26. Brain Drain

Now it was a race—can I get home with my brain intact? Maybe even keeping up the charade that I'm OK?

A smaller bus took those of us heading home to the Leonardo da Vinci – Fiumicino Airport outside of Rome. We had little snacks in our backpack, but nothing about today's schedule would have any sense of regularity. Tour guide Lorna put us in line, and said she wouldn't be allowed to go any further, so we said good-bye to her and went into the passenger-only section. We were way too early, so we gathered in small groups, and I went with one for coffee. It didn't matter which group I was with; I was in battle mode just to survive. Every little thing now was causing me to redouble my efforts. Finding my passport, looking for change. When we finally did get into the boarding lines, it was "hurry up and wait," in long lines for the baggage checking.

That's where I did something rather unique. Members of our group were scattered in line with others, including Italians. Several folks behind me were American.

I hadn't said more than a few words to anyone I knew in the past week. But I knew I had to try. You see, I was supposed to be in a phone interview once I got to Kennedy Airport in New York! What a strange set of occurrences led up to that. And I didn't even know if I could do it. So I approached the woman behind me as gracefully as I could, and began to talk.

She was great. She didn't say anything; she just let me talk as best I could. I tried my best to make full sentences, but often had to grope for words. It was the first time I had tried to talk at length. I soon told her I had said more to her than anyone else in recent days.

And now I knew that something was seriously wrong.

Still, I just didn't want to talk to my tour friends about it. And my seat was adjacent to our tourists on the airplane to New York. So it was back into silent mode, watching movies and sleeping whenever possible (if you can really call that sleep). As we moved west, time stood still because we were following the sun … it literally was a 48-hour day.

In New York, we landed for what was supposed to be a routine 3-hour stopover. I tried to dial the company that was doing the interview, but I couldn't get my cell phone to cooperate. I had missed the interview; but in retrospect, it was better to have missed it all, than to try and not be able to complete a sentence.

Then the weather got bad. I was sitting in a gate for an extra hour, then two. We switched gates two times. Finally, we were given a chance to board, only to wait another hour on the tarmac. We were now going to be 4½ hours late, arriving in San Francisco at 3 a.m., not the original 10:30 p.m. Still, I knew my job wasn't done. There was a van, driven by me only once, waiting for me at the El Rancho Best Western Inn in Millbrae, with which I would drive three of the ladies home. One lived in Woodland, to a place I hadn't been before. And it was raining.

We got off the plane and I went back into my tour guide mode; helping the ladies with their bags. We called for the shuttle—with me hiding my problem with numbers from them as best I could. The shuttle finally arrived, and took us to the El Rancho, where we boarded the van.

Fortunately, at 4 a.m., there aren't a lot of other cars on the road. I took them across the Hayward Bridge, and then just

Melanoma Melodrama

missed the turn off to 680, but I had to get off anyway for a bathroom stop. Back on 680, I had trouble with the window-washer, so I got off to figure that one out. By the time I got to Woodland, it was almost morning. There was a glitch with the directions, but that might have happened anyway. Still, I persevered and found the highway back home, where I deposited my fellow passengers at their own doorsteps. I sighed with relief.

Then I went home.

My wife had expected me the night before. She was taking our son to school. She knew something was amiss from the first time she saw me. After she dropped off my son, she called the doctor, and let me take a nap. I slept until the appointment time.

Dr. Eswaran, my old East Indian friend and G.P., saw me and cringed. The right hand side of my mouth was drooping as if I had Bell's palsy, but he knew my melanoma history. He tried to get me to say, or even write, my problem. I couldn't.

"Go to Mercy General," he said. "Right now."

* * * *

I hadn't been to Mercy General as a patient. And when I went, I didn't expect to be there another ten days—the same length of time I had just spent away from home.

In the emergency waiting room, I read magazines and waited for my turn. Eventually they checked me in, and ordered a CAT scan. More waiting; then into the machine.

What happened next was a scene from Dante's Inferno. They showed me the scan of the tumor, on the screen, from different sectional perspectives. It was huge. The septum dividing the halves of my brain was skewed way over due to the size of the tumor.

The ER doctor looked at me like this was it. Surgery would never get it all. Still, some people choose the brain surgery, with all of its problems and complications, just to have a few more months to live. Others choose, at this point, to do nothing, and eventually die.

They gave me the same choices.

I chose to live.

* * * *

It was midnight. They gave me medication to reduce the swelling and stop the oppressive work of the tumor. I was on a gurney in the hallway of the emergency ward; there were no places in the hospital. So there I lay.

At 2:30 a.m., I realized I wasn't going to get a room this way. I got up and went back to the desk, to ask (nicely) about a room. There were none, according to the clerks behind the desk.

I started back to the gurney in the hallway. I was about to try to sleep, but suddenly I decided it was time to begin my silent but positive advocacy for my health. Clerks don't run the whole hospital. So I went back in front of the desk, and stood there, waiting. My being there made them nervous.

"I'm waiting for a room," I said.

That set the clerks (who work under the doctors) to work. Soon, the other doctors came over and asked me what was wrong. One of the doctors showed me a room where he could move my gurney in the meantime, and within an hour, they had moved me in the best ward in the hospital.

I was on my way; I wasn't going to die in the ER hallway. Not only that, the night nurse was gorgeous and friendly. I was on Italy time, so I stayed up talking to her.

I did everything I could to make myself noticeable. I wanted that surgery, but they couldn't schedule one for another week. I had to wait in line. After my nice little escape, they moved me to "Neuro"—a place not so nice, on a busy hallway, with problem roommates.

The temporary drugs (steroids) were working, and I still had a lot more of my physical body attuned to reality than most of the other patients. I dressed normally, went to the cafeteria, got full meals, a shower, etc., and visited with many guests. The bishop stopped by, and quite a few well-wishers from the church family came by with balloons, CDs and games.

Sunday was my son's 13th birthday. Every year, we wake up the birthday person with the Mexican song, "Las Mañanitas," with guitars, candles and gifts. It was the first time I had missed that—but I was there by cell phone. Our daughter, a sophomore at NYU, was also there by phone, leaving Becky no hands to manage all the gifts! A peer-group rock-climbing birthday party had been postponed.

The doctors either had to do surgery soon, or let me out to go home, and come back later. By Tuesday, they made their decision: the surgery would be done on Thursday; I would stay in the Neuro ward until then.

When you're out in the normal medical world and you need to see some cancer specialists, you know who you're going to see, and then have your questions ready when you see them. But in the hospital, you don't know who's coming when. You're asleep; two women come in to my room—they look the same. One is there to take out the trash. The other is Dr. Susan Lee, from radiological services. And you have a mind that isn't doing too well on names right now. How can you prepare? It was hard to keep track of them all. Lots of doctors and nurses came in at all hours of the day and night—in fact, there is no day and night in the hospital.

I called some friends, including Suellen Rowlison, my medical advocate from the first surgery. I wanted to know if there was anything I should write down on the consent form for surgery. But by the end of the call, she was on her way down, again, to be my medical advocate during the surgery.

On Thursday, October 18, 2007, I was wheeled away to the surgery room. No more skin and muscle and lymph. We're going into the brain now. This is it.

* * * *

Dr. Yen came in and did a miracle.

* * * *

When I was awakened, there were my wife, son and Suellen. How great it is to see your friends and family at that moment.

Especially since you feel naked; you feel voiceless; you feel like you're about to go to the bathroom. You don't know about the catheter, or that there are sheets on you. When they asked what I wanted, the first word that came out of my mouth was "Lipitor!" I don't even take that, but it was one of the last words spoken by my wife before I woke up! What I really wanted was ice chips or lemon drops in my mouth to make it human.

Still, I could tell Dr. Yen had done a fantastic job. I was back in the business of life—he had removed "all of the tumor that he could see." I was eternally grateful.

Now I was in the recovery business: two more nights in the ICU—the second because there was no room back in the main ward. I was still strapped into my bed by the monitors. For two days I could only see a portion of the entry area outside. Finally a nurse could see I was the most able-bodied patient by far. He got me unhooked and took me for a walk. Then he got me a room in Neuro—allowing me to walk (and push the wheelchair) rather than ride!

Melanoma Melodrama

Back in the Neuro ward I was in a tight room with still another problem roommate. I had to get home.

The morning of Sunday the 21st, Dr. Yen was coming in. I knew he'd be early. Not a problem: I'm still on Italy time! He came in at 6:45 a.m. I was ready—in my chair with a list of questions. He answered them, and signed a release.

There was still plenty to do. My wife came in around 8:00 a.m. We took care of medications, talked to another doctor, and waited for the release. Finally, it came. A nurse pushed my chair to the car, and that was it.

It was so good to be going home—a place I wasn't sure I would ever make it back to. Ironically, the place was a mess—a leak behind the tiles in the shower had ballooned into a plumbing leak and the shower and bathroom were in total disrepair. The front door wouldn't work. No Internet.

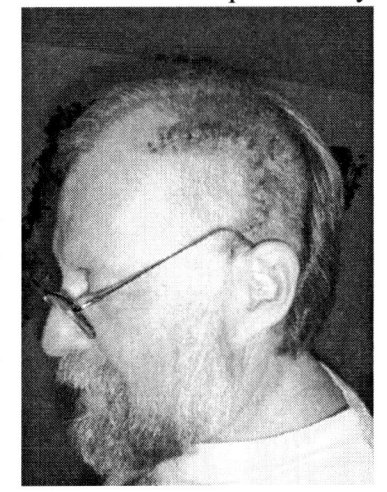

But I was home.

I had to get the "hospital off of me." I still had electrode marks on my skin from all of the monitors. I still had stool-softeners in me, as well as being on steroids and anti-blackout drugs. My new scar looked like the *upper*-case version of *gamma*. My hair reminded my family of "Foghorn Leghorn."

It didn't matter. I was home.

* * * *

It was so different from my first surgery, when pains had kept me down every step of the way. This time, my body was working well. On Tuesday we went for a walk in the local American River Parkway—that was like heaven.

Chuck Myer

I still had plenty of medical work to do: I kept a previously established appointment with Dr. Rohatgi on Wednesday. He set up a PET scan for me. I was also needed in radiology to set up for the whole-brain radiation in November.

My speech only got better and better—soon the only missing words might be late at night when I was tired (something that might have happened anyway). Each day, I used cryptograms, jumbles and crosswords to regain my strength in those areas. I had always been good at them, but in the hospital, I noticed a huge slip in my abilities. After the surgery, it took about ten days, but I kept at it. Each day, I got stronger and stronger, until I was virtually back up to the level I was at before.

A week after surgery, my old Italian class was meeting to discuss the art and architecture of Italy. I had previously promised the teacher I would share from my trip. I had 3 CDs now of my slides; but would I be able to talk about art and architecture without betraying my brain problem? And if I am specifically dealing with things that I had been dealing with while I had the tumor, my brain gets a little foggy. I went; and did my best.

My mother and brother came up to see me; they were so glad to see me up and around and making jokes about it.

That weekend, we had the "rescheduled" peer group party for my son Tim. I was able to go and watch for three hours as the kids climbed up and down the artificial "granite arches" with ropes and tethers, and then enjoyed their pizza, cokes and presents. (Again, the scene from "Our Town", with Emily asking if she can go back down to life to a birthday party, came to my consciousness.)

I went to get my fourth PET scan. But this one was a little more intense. Besides being thrown into the tube, this time I was wearing my new radiation mask, and had an IV feeding into my arm. (I didn't even mind listening to "Red Roses for a Blue Lady," and "Tammy.")

Halloween. Again, my surgical scars are going to win the prize. Some high-school age trick-or-treaters saw my scar—when I said, "That's just my make-up," they didn't believe it.

I "needed to do something with my hair." It was November now, time for a new month of recovery. A woman named Mary Ann Becker, 46, had cut my hair twice at the American Cancer Society Relay for Life in 2005 and 2006. She often gave to cancer events. She'd be perfect. But she had just died.

I still had her card, and found the salon still in operation. The woman who answered, Debbie, said she'd be happy to cut my hair (or at least the half that hadn't been cut.) So, on November 1 I had the rest of my hair cut down to the level where my hair had come back around the scar, with a hint of a "Mohawk" on the top. That really helped.

I tried to pay her, but she just shook her head.

There are a lot of great folks out there.

On the 18th day after surgery, I went to see Dr. Yen in his regular office. What a great man. He was so happy to see me "back"—to a place he hadn't known me before. He asked me to keep talking while he took out the staples! And he surprised me by saying I could drive again.

Next came three weeks of radiation. Another mask, but this time it was the whole brain, not just a spot on the neck. Dr. Lee and her staff were excellent. Side effects, of course. But I'm a veteran now.

So I feel great (is it the steroids?)—every day is a wonder, and I'm very happy to be here. And yet, the actuarial tables give me a very short lifespan. Most melanoma patients with a recurrent phase to the brain are considered about to die. One more little tumor could do it.

But I am here enjoying my life and my recovery to the fullest. Do I go back to work like nothing happened? Or do I retire early, arrange my will and prepare for the end?

So the ultimate rhetorical question is this: Shall I use my time to prepare to die? Or prepare to live?

My oncologist, Dr. Rohatgi, who is in this business, can only say, "nobody knows." And Dr. Eswaran, my G.P., the man of few words, just said this:

"Life goes on."

* * * *

So here I am. No hair. Standing before (my) God.

I feel great. But I'm publishing the book now, just in case the actuarial tables are right.

I know now that the rest of my life will be spent fighting this thing. "Winning" and "losing" become just a matter of time…

If you live five years from cancer surgery, you have a chance… Four years, and 11 months to go…

27. A Better Person

This is a hard concept to try to explain. It sounds really strange to say, but since I've had cancer, I've been in great health. The other nagging chronic problems I was dealing with (asthma, hypertension, acid reflux, hiatal hernia, high cholesterol, and weight issues) haven't all vanished entirely, but every one of them has shown marked improvement since my cancer biopsy. Perhaps they just seem to pale in comparison with the new situation.

I'm slimmer, and I feel better and stronger (except while dealing with the other side effects, of course). I haven't had a cold or the flu for a long time. When I was in Italy, my brain may have been a bit baffled, but the rest of me was in top form.

There's something about cancer that actually improves your life. It can test you, and challenge you to become a better person.

Perhaps you remember when Lance Armstrong tried to explain it. I didn't believe it either.

He told Oprah Winfrey, and he wrote in his book, "I never would have won the Tour de France if I hadn't had cancer first." Right.

Lance had testicular cancer that metastasized to his lungs and brain—and that helped him win the world's most grueling bike race? It reminds me of General Westmoreland's claim about having to destroy the Vietnamese village in order to save it.

But there's something about a crisis like this that weeds out your life, and instantly rearranges everything in it according to the "real" priority order—not the priority order you had been giving it.

Another example is when the forest rangers tell us that forest fires (at least those that start through natural causes like lightning) can be good for the forest. The natural processes of fire burn out the dangerous buildup of undergrowth that can ultimately be more deadly to the forest than periodic natural fires.

My life had a lot of underbrush—a lot of things that weren't in priority order. The cancer diagnosis was a wake-up call that led to a lot of self-searching and behavioral changes. All of a sudden a lot of things that I had been "putting off" started moving up to the front burner.

I didn't jump out of any airplanes, but I did have an appreciation for the lyrics in the country song about the reaction to a cancer diagnosis sung by Tim McGraw, "Live like you were dying":

I went skydiving
I went rocky mountain climbing
I went 2.7 seconds on a bull named Fu Manchu
I loved deeper and I spoke sweeter
And I gave forgiveness I've been denying
Someday I hope you get the chance
To live like you were dying

I'm an actor. I've been involved in community and educational theater groups for 35 years. I even had a recent "paid gig," when my services as an actor translated into paychecks and income tax withholding.

Suppose you're an actor on a hit television series. There's a crack team of writers, and every week you are at their mercy trusting them to come up with a good story line for your character. And you hope the Nielsen ratings are showing public interest in your character so it doesn't get written off the show.

Then, like Nancy on *thirtysomething* or Lynette on *Desperate Housewives*, the writers decide that your character is going to get cancer.

What do you do?

You jump for joy, that's what. That's an actor's dream. Pathos. Raw emotion. Exploration of the spirit. All of a sudden, the camera lens is going to be close up on you. Every facial expression, tear, smile, and grimace is going to be magnified as never before. Surely your name will come up at Emmy time. Even if your character dies, they'll never forget you—and your performance.

Well, like I said, I'm an actor. And I'm not saying I'm glad this happened to me. But it's the role I've been given, and I'm going to make the most of it.

Things are different now, and always will be. Whenever I see things tempting me back into my old life routine, I stop and remember: Life as I know it is over. I might as well start building a better one.

So now I must decide what steps to take—the decision is mine. It's not just a matter of "searching" for some pre-ordained plan for my life. Instead, I see life as a series of choices—we just want to make the wise choice.

There are those whose catastrophic illnesses have given them a new identity, and perhaps a greater calling than they had previously. Chris Reeve comes to mind. His death, and that of his wife (a non-smoking victim of lung cancer), are tragic losses, but with a positive outcome for the rest of us.

Is there a way for me to translate my experiences as a positive role model for other melanoma or cancer patients? In a way, I'm hoping this book will be a step in that direction.

A PSA from the 70s showed a hippie couple singing a song called "Fear, Guilt and Pain." When I spend precious time with my family, I now try to remember: We don't have time for fear, guilt, or pain; we only have time for love.

2008 Update

This is a story I'll never be able to finish, but I can try to keep it updated!

I've always said, in California, while waiting for our disasters, at least we have great weather! 2008. Feeling great, with a body still in good shape and feeling much better than I had during the "Interferon year." But the stakes are so much higher. For a person with "recurrent" melanoma, everything's on the line, and the odds are tough. It wasn't long until the MRIs found that the melanoma wasn't stopping. In January, I found that I had four more "spots"—small brain tumors. My oncologist recommended that I should try the high-tech "gamma-knife" radiation procedure (mentioned in Chapter 10). By the time I was scheduled, the number of "spots" was up to eight. I needed the equipment much longer than originally thought.

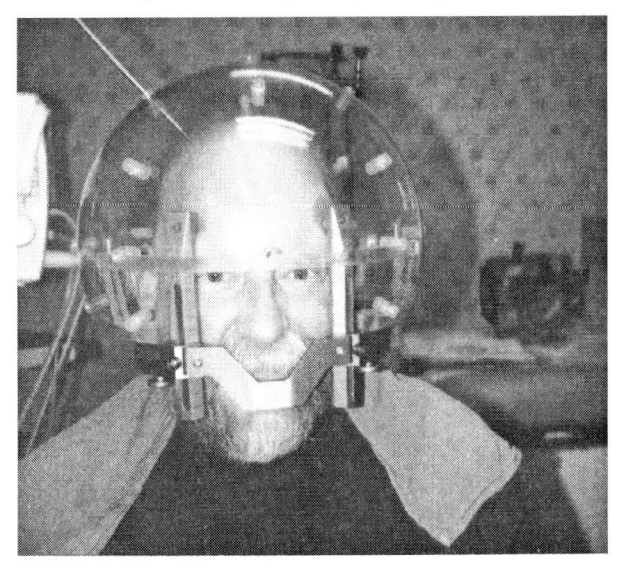

In February I had another PET scan. This one found cancer

in other organs: my spleen and right adrenal gland. (I'll have to Google them to find out where they are.) A new pill treatment: Temodar. A five-day series of pills that cost $1200! Not to mention the pill you take just to prepare for the Temodar, and its long list of side effects.

Still, all of these measures are basically "palliative"—no doctor ever promised a cure. So now I'm in a time of closure with my family, my "retired clergy" job and friends. I just turned 54, and will start to pull in whatever retirement I have coming to my family. My hope is for a period of a "medical retirement," hopefully long, and peaceful, not painful, for those around me. But I've already lived beyond the average length of time following recurrence of this disease—still relatively unknown and, for the most part, incurable at this stage. Whatever we can do to study melanoma, we must, particularly if it is related to climate change. Too many lives are in danger.

Don't forget to use the sun-block.

About the Author

Chuck Myer is an urban planner, free-lance writer, playwright, and a consultant to arts, government, and religious organizations. He is described by many as a "Renaissance Man."

Born in Puerto Rico and raised in the San Francisco (East) Bay Area, he has a degree in City and Regional Planning, and has worked for eight California cities and counties. He served the City of Gilroy for over fifteen years as Senior Planner and Public Information Officer.

As an actor and musician, Myer has appeared in over thirty theatrical productions, and performs with the Sacramento Capitolaires barbershop chorus. His original plays have been produced by Motherlode Stage Company, Gilroy and Roseville High Schools, Sacramento Religious Community for Peace, and Methodist Actors Serving the Church.

Myer serves as executive officer of the Retired Clergy Association for the California-Nevada United Methodist Church, for which his wife, Becky Goodwin, is a pastor. They have two children, Holly, a college sophomore, 19, and 13-year-old Timothy, an eighth-grader.